Understanding **Fractions** *Visually*
Second Edition

Easy,
logically
ordered
and
illustrated

with

basic **shapes**,

equations

etc.

		Page(s)
Introduction to Fractions		4 – 7
Halving and Quartering		8 – 29
Equivalent Fractions		30 – 33
Halves	$\frac{1}{2}$ s	34
Quarters	$\frac{1}{4}$ s	35 - 36
Comparing	$\frac{1}{2}$ s and $\frac{1}{4}$ s	37
Eighths	$\frac{1}{8}$ s	38 – 39
Comparing	$\frac{1}{4}$ s and $\frac{1}{8}$ s	40 – 41
Comparing	$\frac{1}{2}$ s $\frac{1}{4}$ s $\frac{1}{8}$ s	42 – 43
Fifths	$\frac{1}{5}$ s	44 – 45
Tenths	$\frac{1}{10}$ s	46 – 48
Quiz 1		49

	Page(s)
Comparing $\frac{1}{5}$ s and $\frac{1}{10}$ s	50 – 52
Thirds $\frac{1}{3}$ s	53
Sixths $\frac{1}{6}$ s	54 – 55
Comparing $\frac{1}{3}$ s and $\frac{1}{6}$ s	56 – 57
Ninths $\frac{1}{9}$ s	58 – 59
Comparing $\frac{1}{6}$ s and $\frac{1}{9}$ s	60 – 61
Comparing $\frac{1}{3}$ s $\frac{1}{6}$ s $\frac{1}{9}$ s	62 – 63
Equivalent Fractions and Decimals	64 – 66
Quiz 2	67
Fractions, Decimals and Percentages	68 – 73
Other Titles	74

Introduction

Once upon a time …

… a mother went to a take-away.

She bought a pizza for her 3 children.

Mum divided the pizza like this.

But the younger boy was NOT happy!

Why was he not happy?

What could be the problem?

Any idea?

That is NOT fair!

The pizzas were swapped
for the younger boy and the older boy.

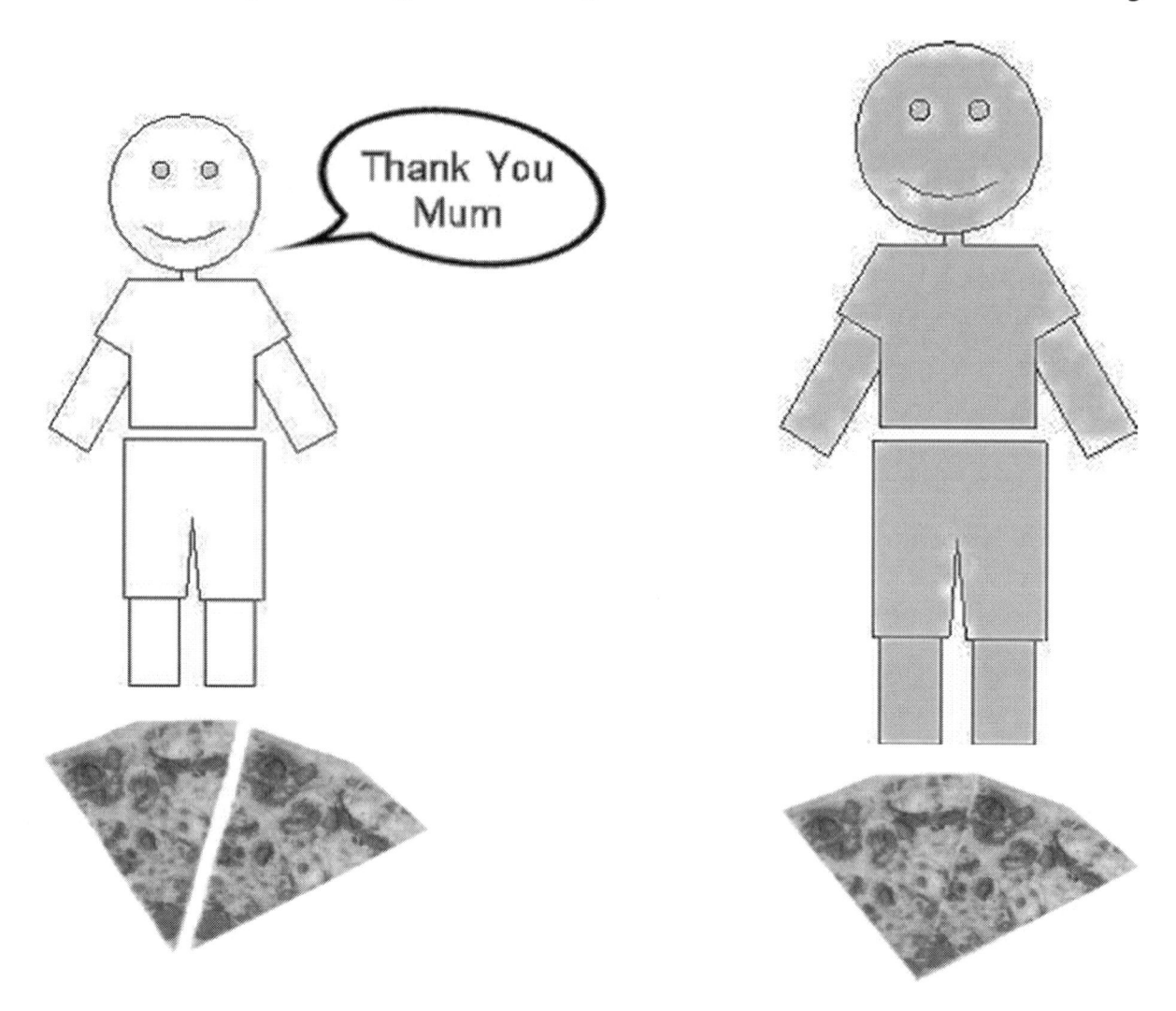

"Thank You Mum"

Then, the younger boy WAS happy!

What was the problem?

What do you think?

Check your answers (and explanation) on page 75.

What is a fraction?
Fraction is a **part** or **parts** of a **whole**.

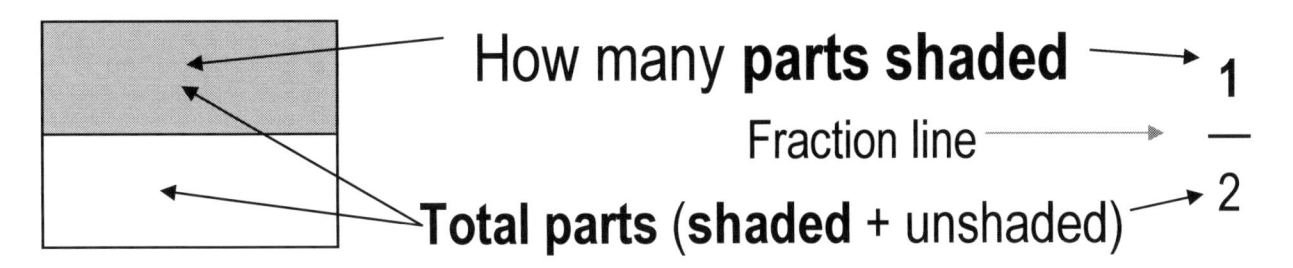

How many **parts shaded** → 1

Fraction line → ―

Total parts (**shaded** + unshaded) → 2

- **Top** number (*numerator*) shows **how many** parts (out of a whole)
- **Bottom** number (*denominator*) means **total** parts (to make whole)

| **One** part is **shaded** out of **two** parts. That is a **half** or **one-half**. | $\dfrac{1}{2}$ |

Also, **one** part is **unshaded** out of **two** parts. That is another **half** or **one-half**. $\dfrac{1}{2}$

And $\dfrac{1}{2}$ + $\dfrac{1}{2}$ = $\dfrac{2}{2}$ = 1

A **fraction** can be: *small,* $\dfrac{1}{8}$, *medium* $\dfrac{1}{2}$ *or* *big;* $\dfrac{7}{8}$

But **not** as **big** as a **whole** like ▨ or ▨ .

- A proper **fraction** is <u>always</u> *smaller* or *less* than a **whole**!

Halving 2, 4

Ali and **Asha** are friends and often share things. For the following shapes, one of them gets the <u>shaded</u> **part** and the other will get the <u>unshaded</u> **part**.

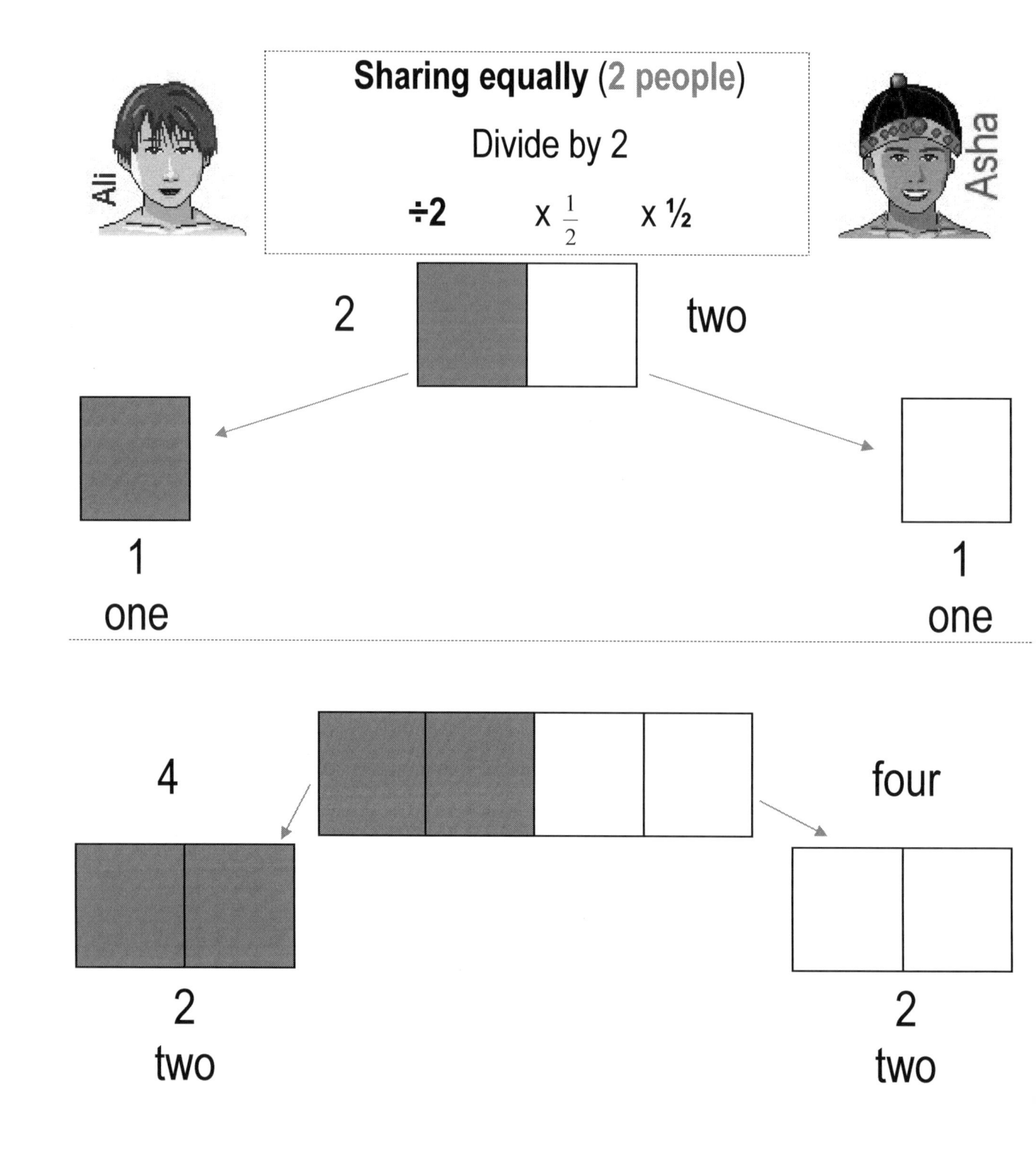

Sharing equally (2 people)

Divide by 2

÷2   × $\frac{1}{2}$ × ½

2   two

1   1
one   one

4   four

2   2
two   two

8

Halving 6, 8

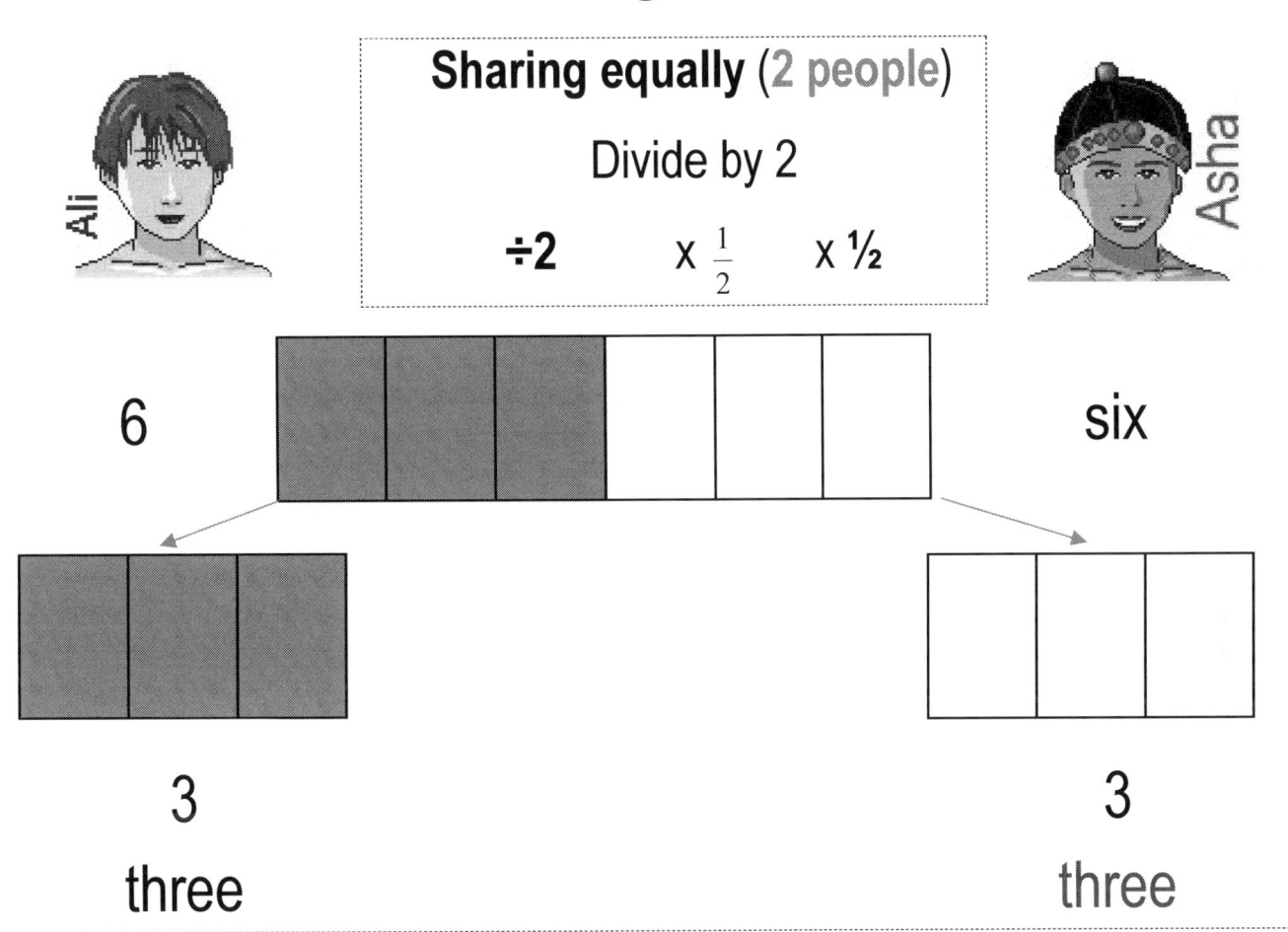

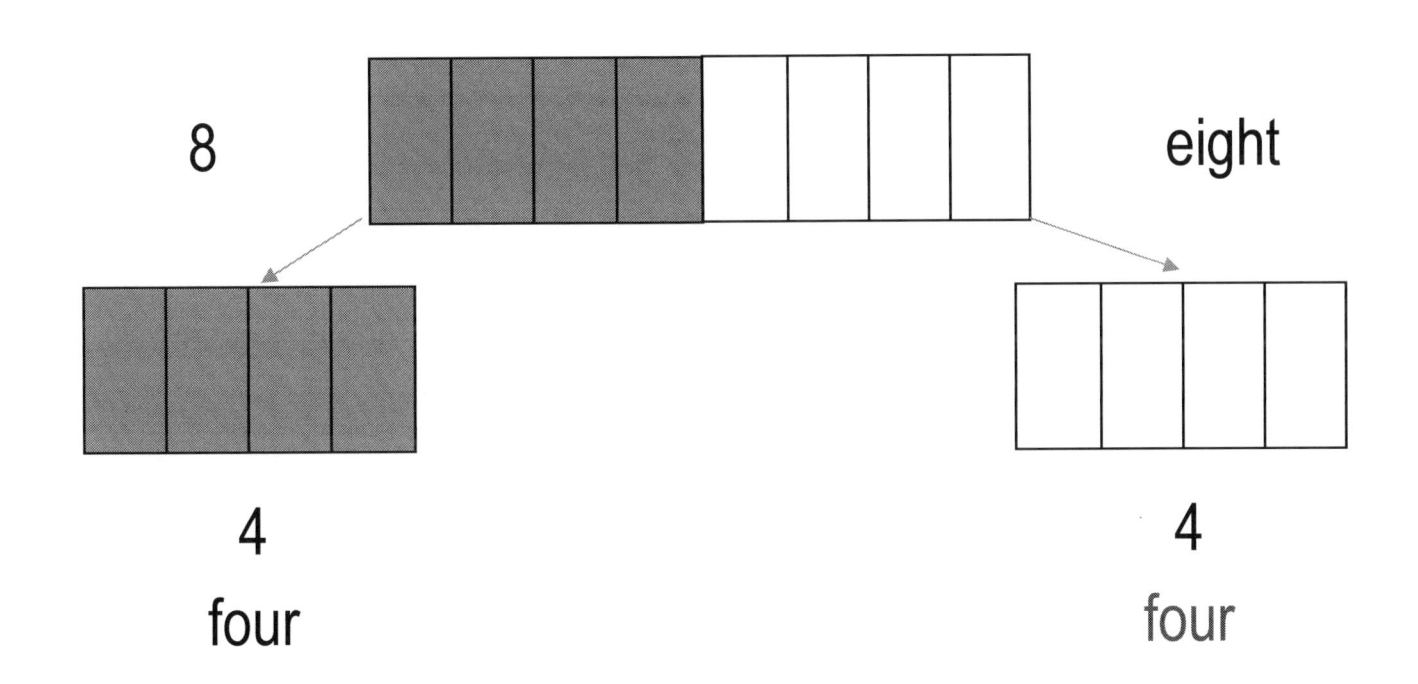

Sharing equally (2 people)

Divide by 2

÷2   x $\frac{1}{2}$ x ½

Ali

Asha

6

six

3

three

3

three

8

eight

4

four

4

four

Halving 10, 12

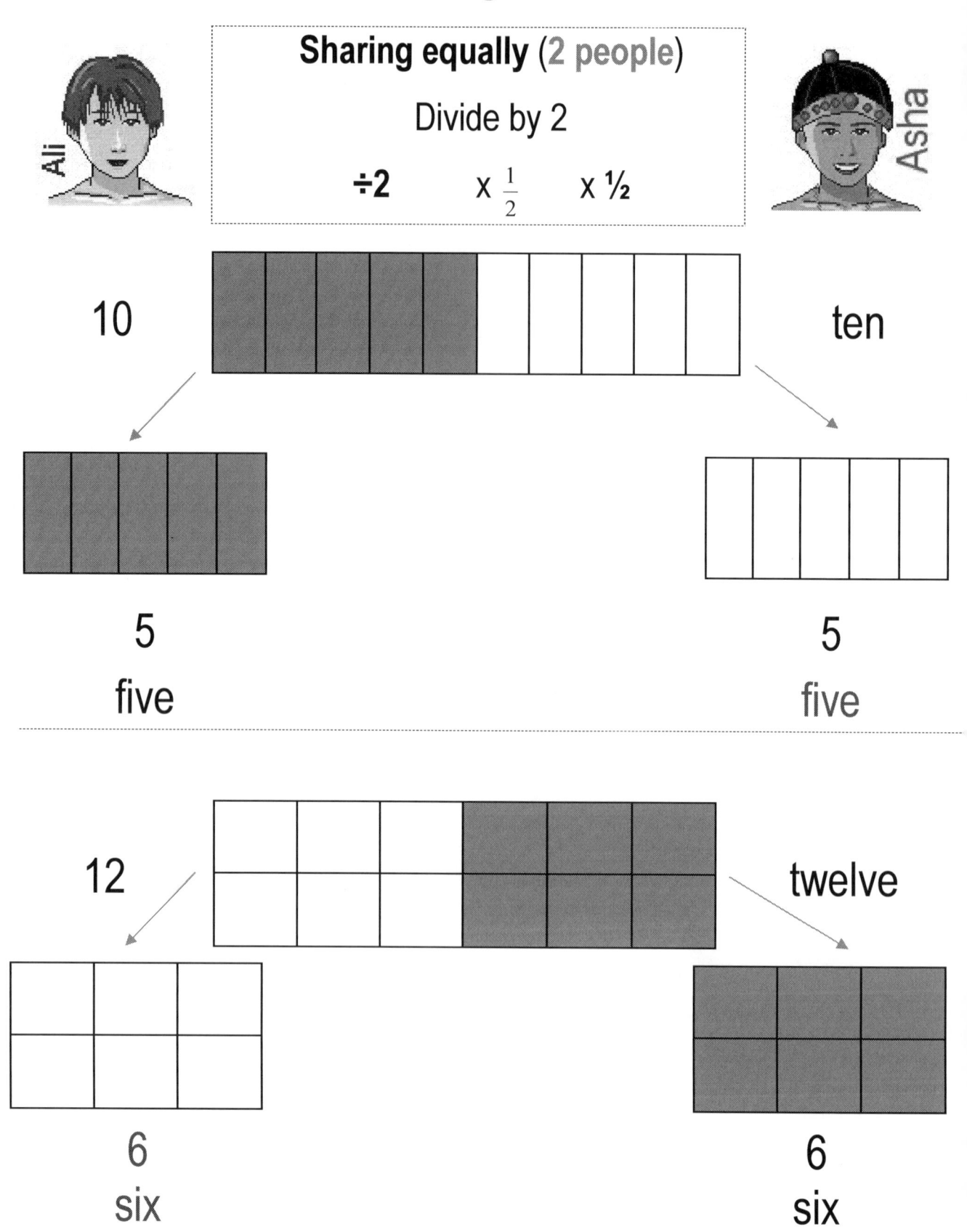

Sharing equally (2 people)

Divide by 2

÷2   x $\frac{1}{2}$ x ½

10 — ten

5 — five

5 — five

12 — twelve

6 — six

6 — six

Halving 14, 16

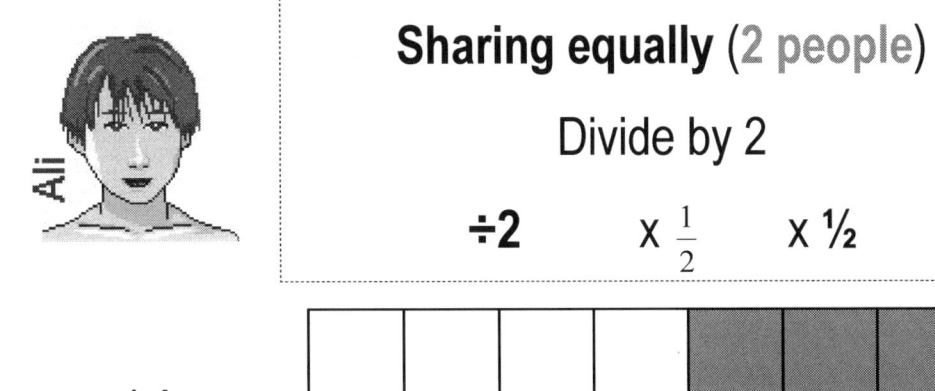

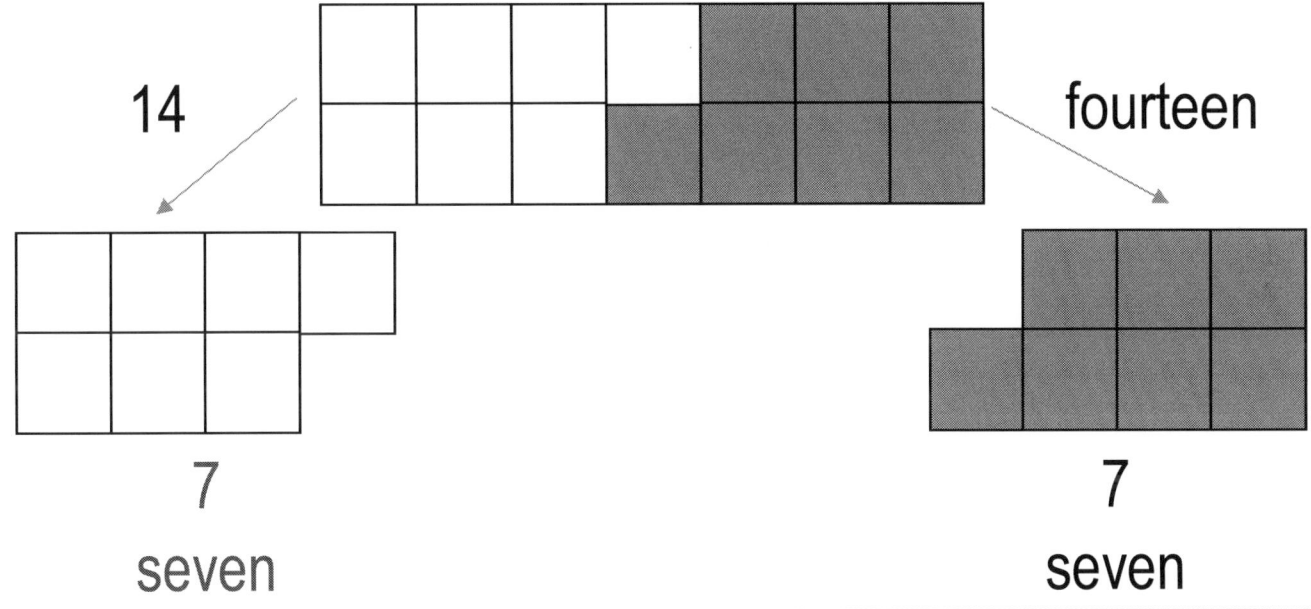

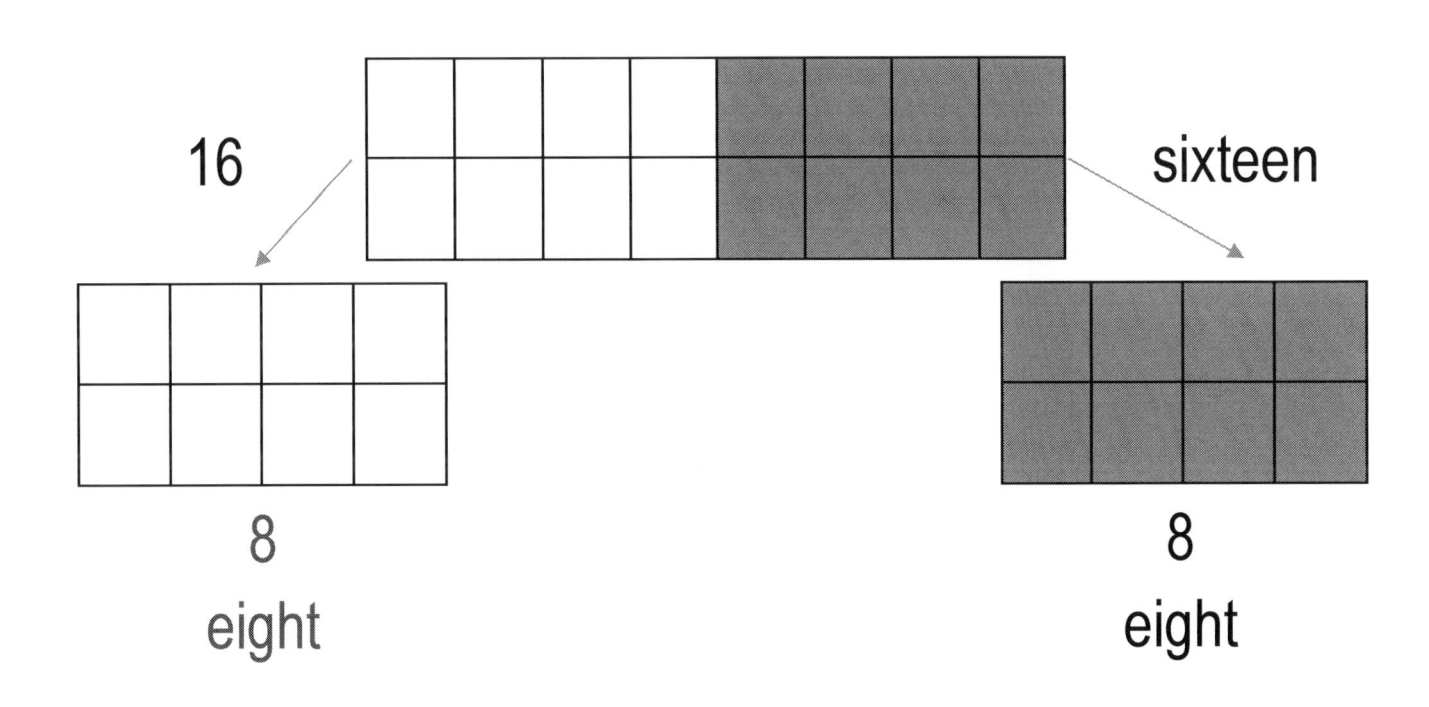

Sharing equally (2 people)

Divide by 2

÷2   x $\frac{1}{2}$ x ½

14 → 7   fourteen → 7
seven   seven

16 → 8   sixteen → 8
eight   eight

Halving 18, 20

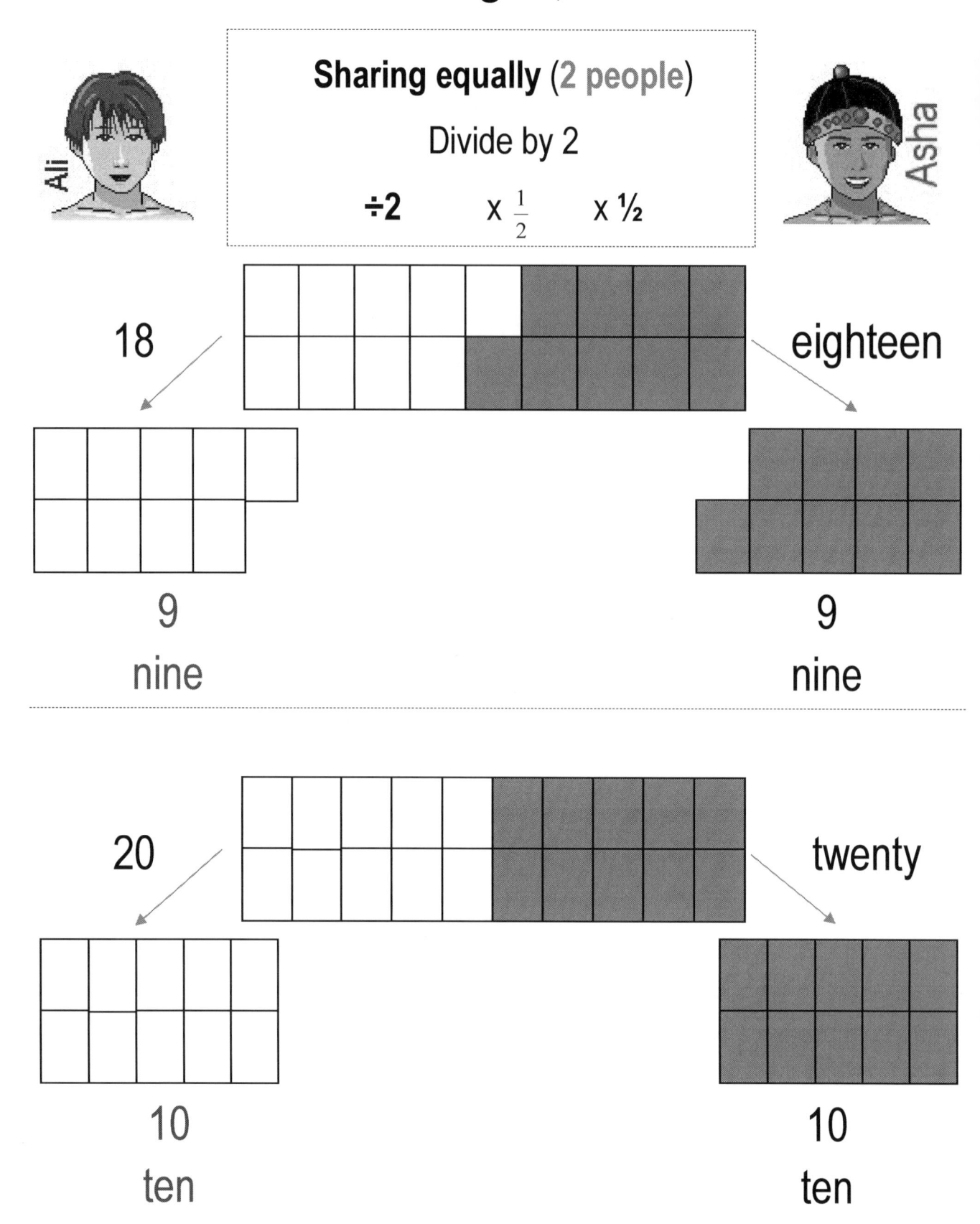

Sharing equally (2 people)

Divide by 2

÷2   x $\frac{1}{2}$ x ½

18 → eighteen

9
nine

9
nine

20 → twenty

10
ten

10
ten

Halving 1, 3

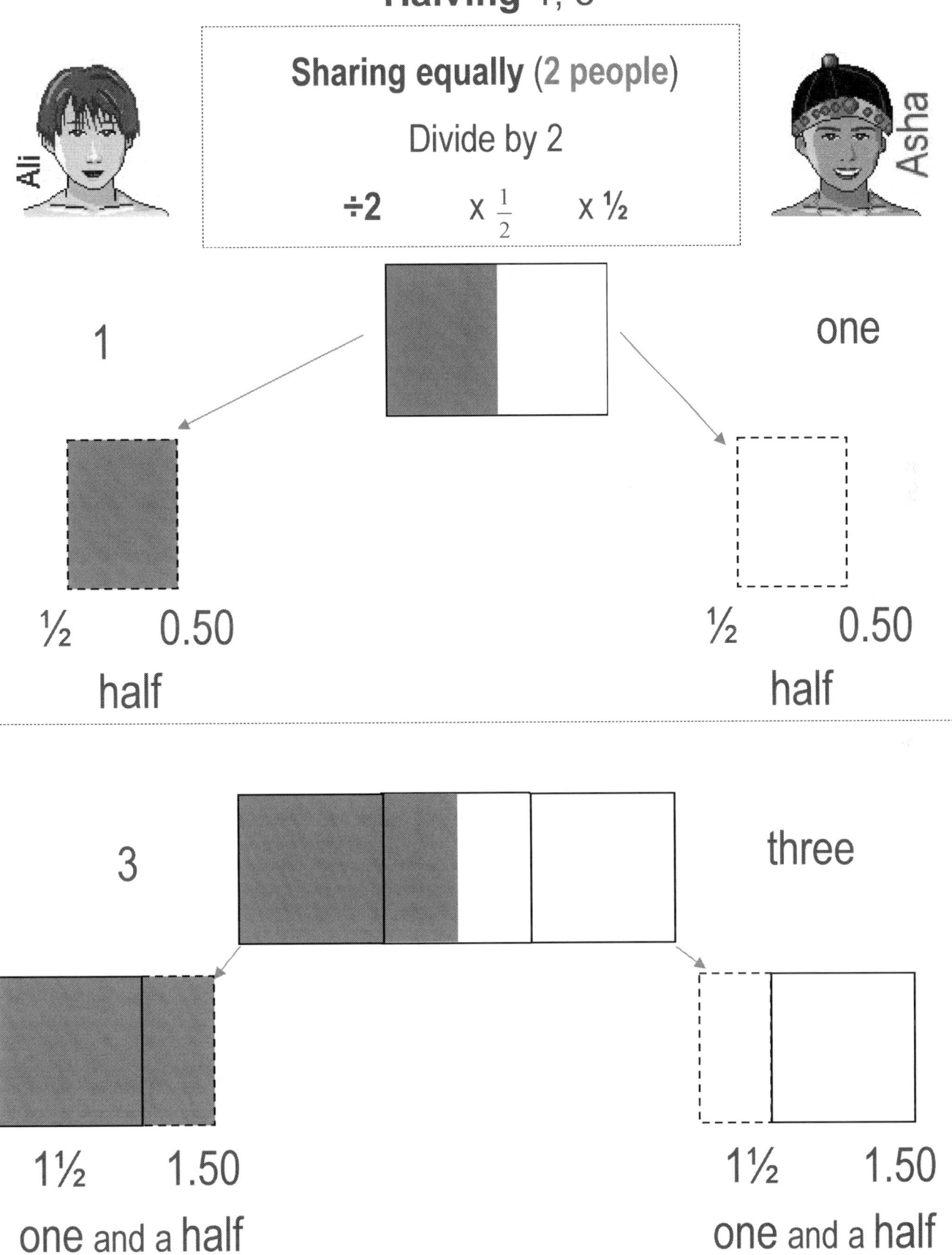

Sharing equally (2 people)

Divide by 2

÷2   x $\frac{1}{2}$ x ½

1 — one

½   0.50
half

½   0.50
half

3 — three

1½   1.50
one and a half

1½   1.50
one and a half

Halving 5, 7

Sharing equally (2 people)

Divide by 2

÷2   x $\frac{1}{2}$ x ½

5

five

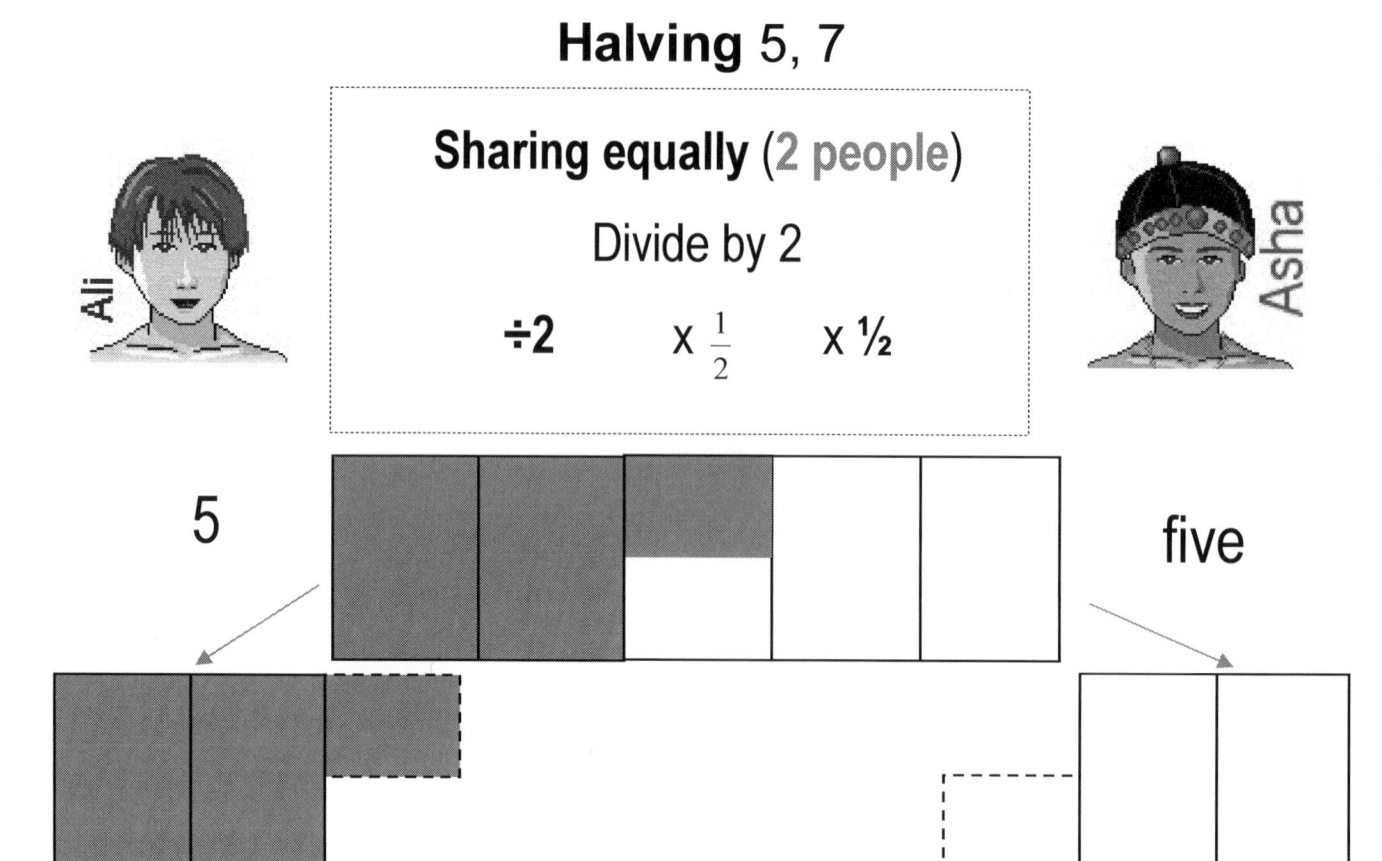

2½   2.50

two and a half

2½   2.50

two and a half

7

seven

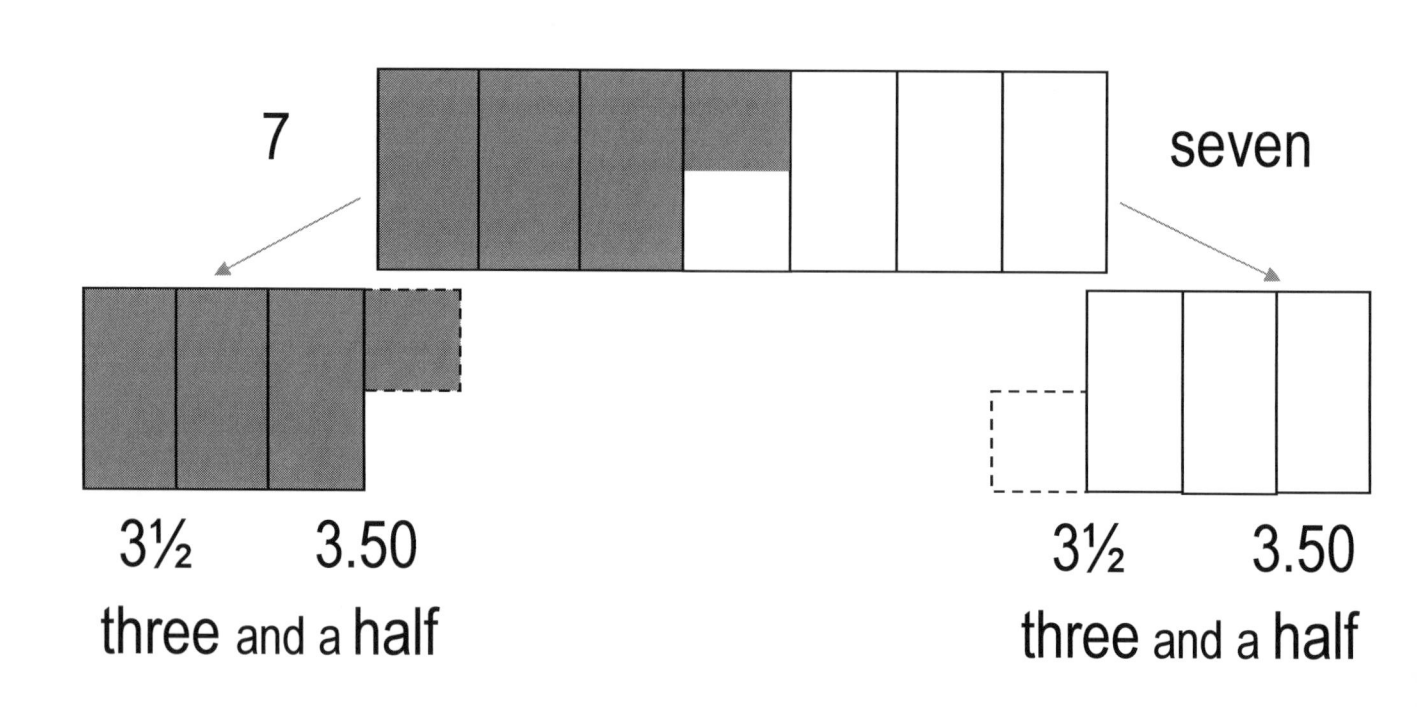

3½   3.50

three and a half

3½   3.50

three and a half

Halving 9, 11

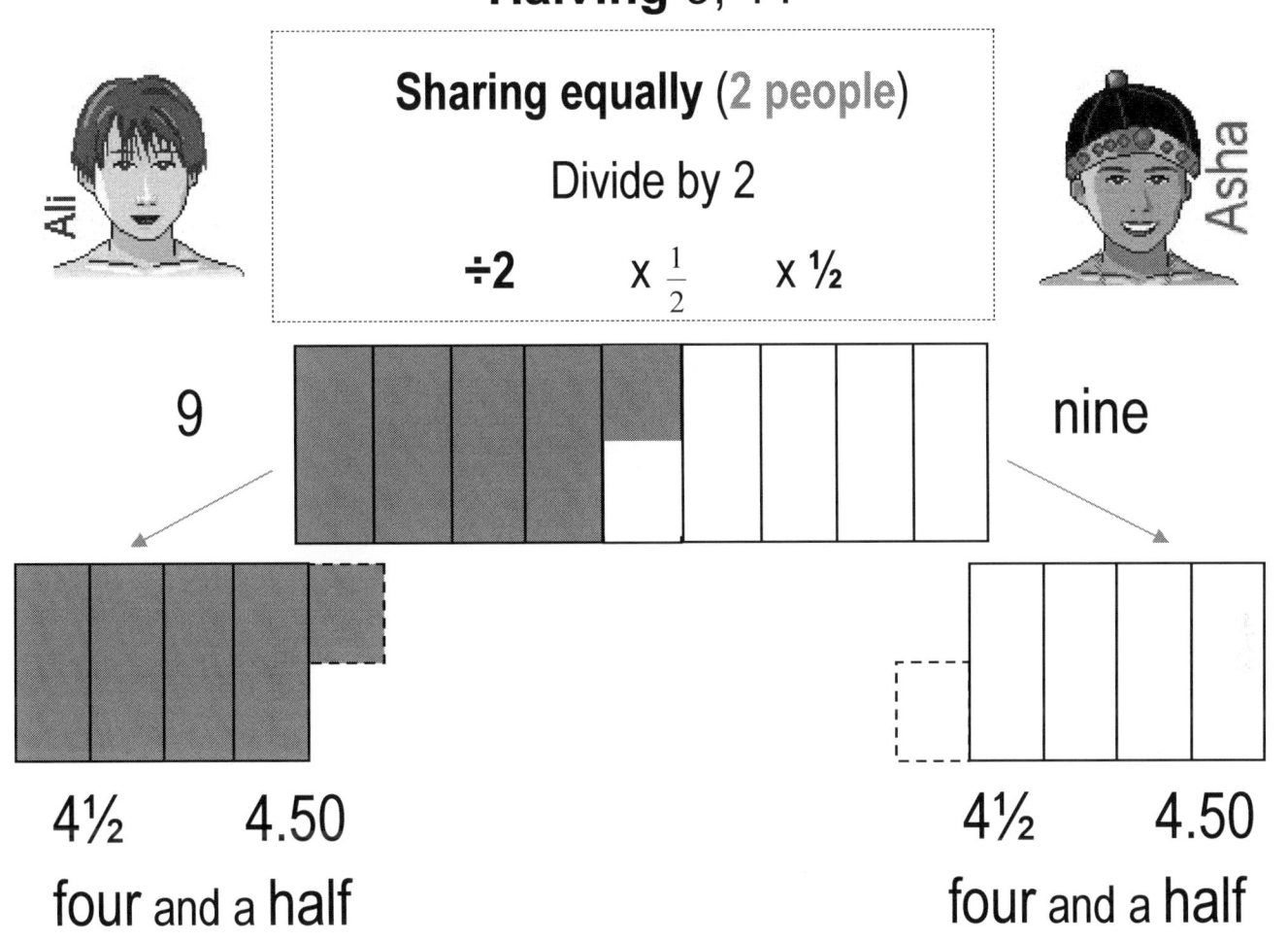

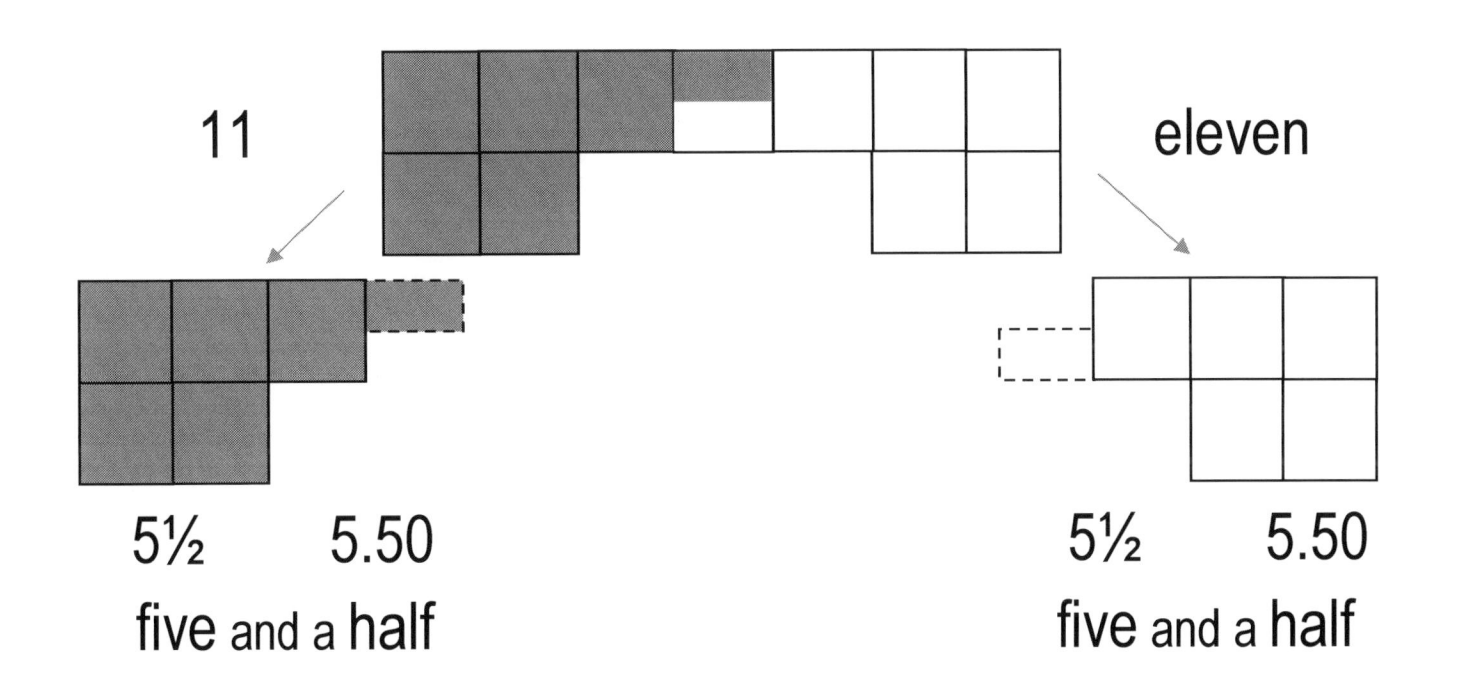

Sharing equally (2 people)

Divide by 2

÷2   x $\frac{1}{2}$ x ½

9   nine

4½   4.50   4½   4.50

four and a half   four and a half

---

11   eleven

5½   5.50   5½   5.50

five and a half   five and a half

Halving 13, 15

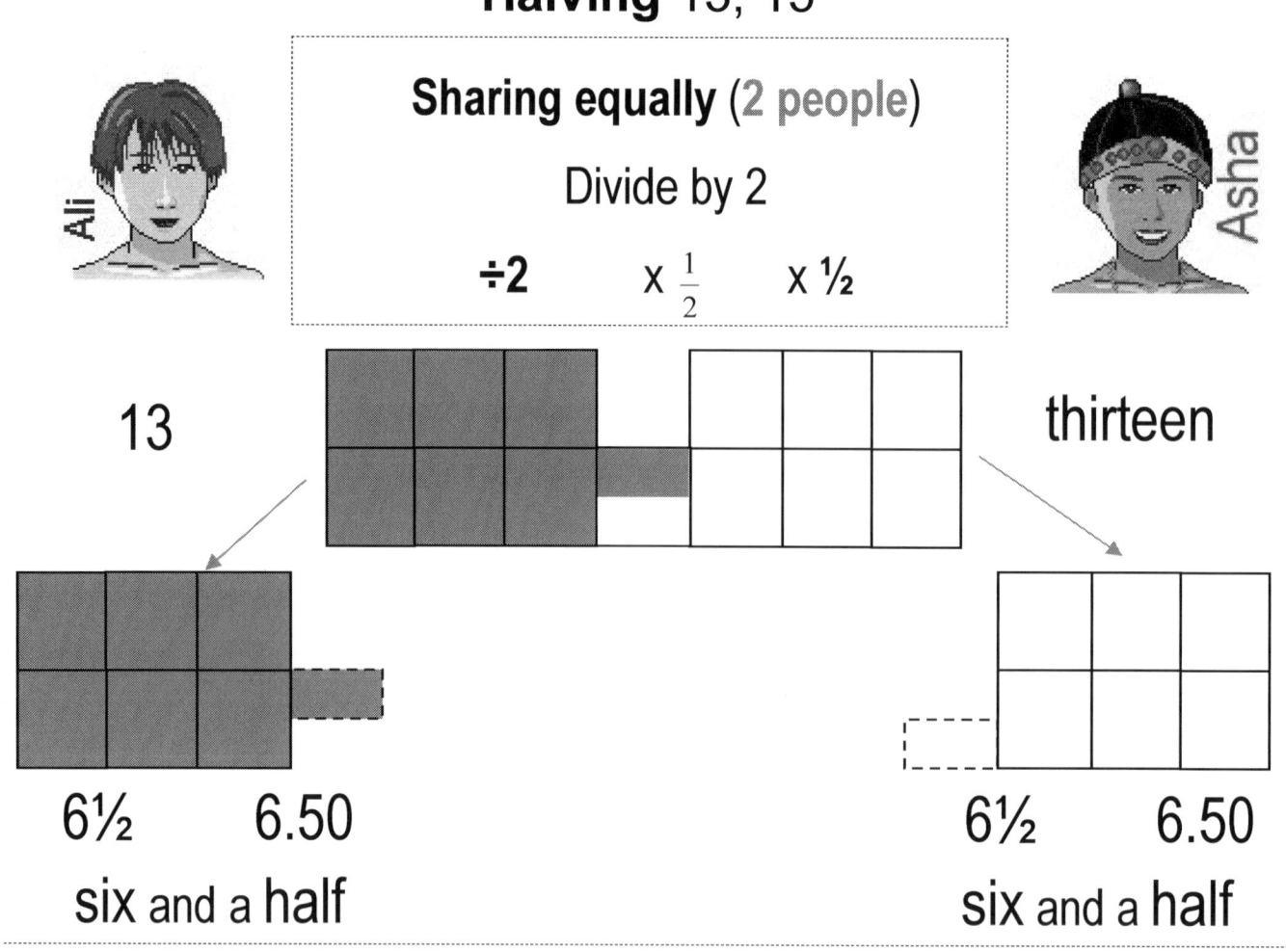

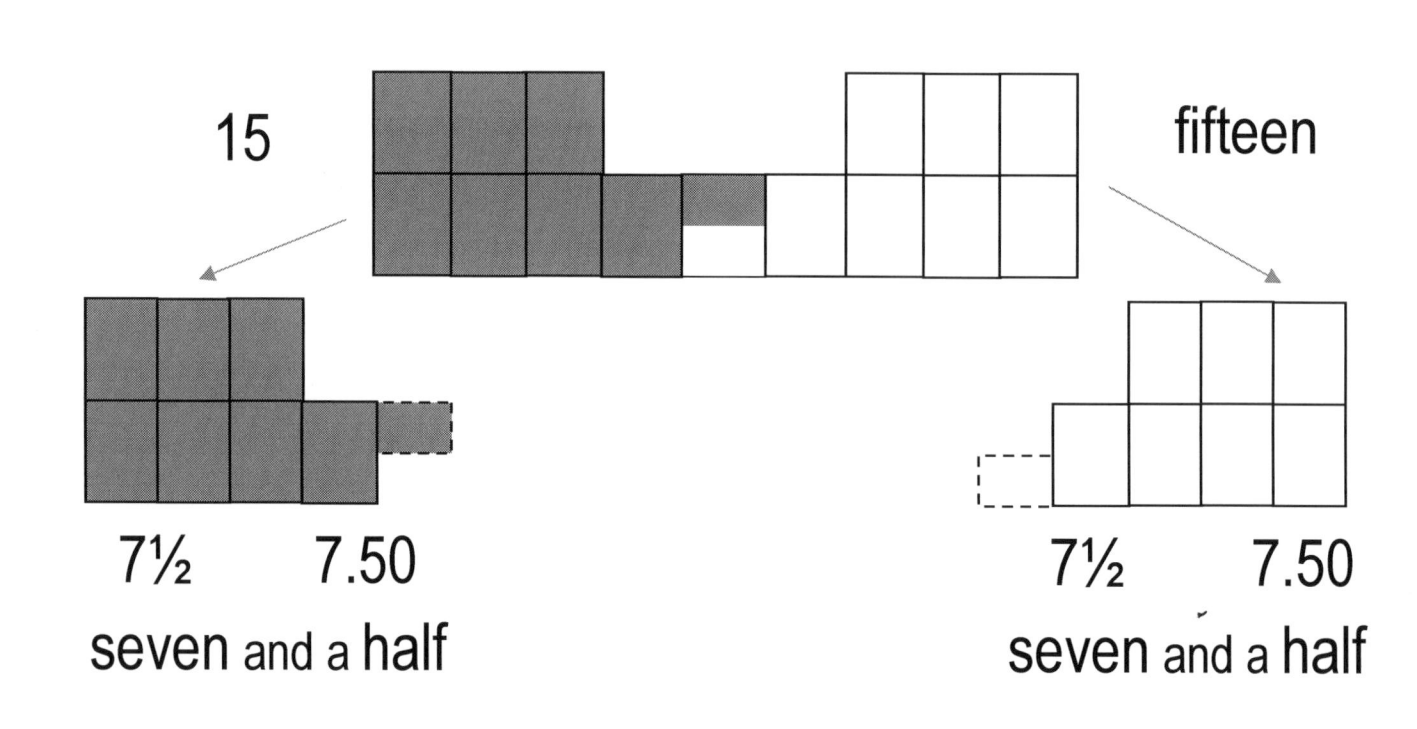

Sharing equally (2 people)

Divide by 2

$\div 2$ $\times \frac{1}{2}$ $\times \frac{1}{2}$

13 thirteen

6½   6.50   6½   6.50
six and a half   six and a half

15 fifteen

7½   7.50   7½   7.50
seven and a half   seven and a half

Halving 17, 19

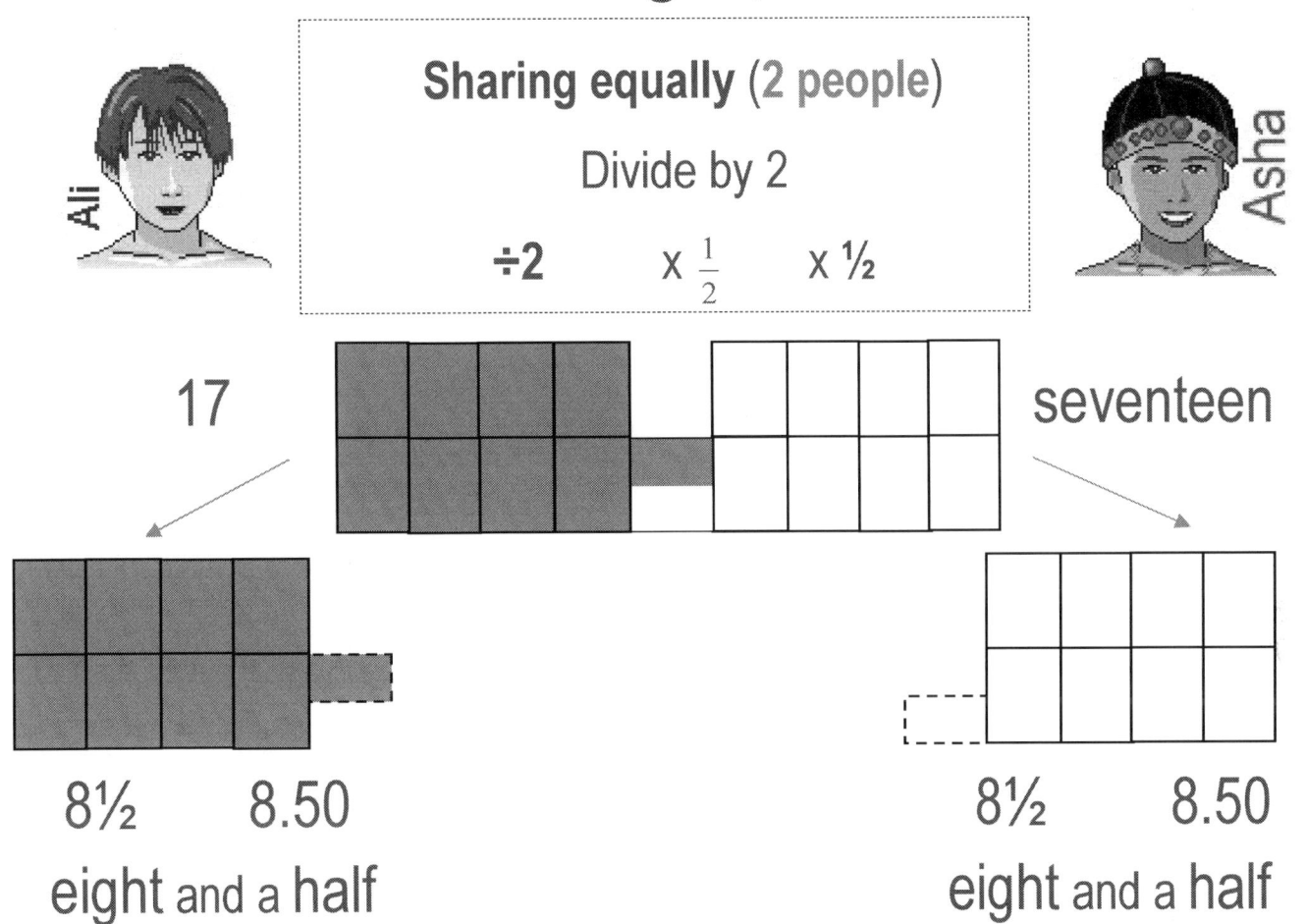

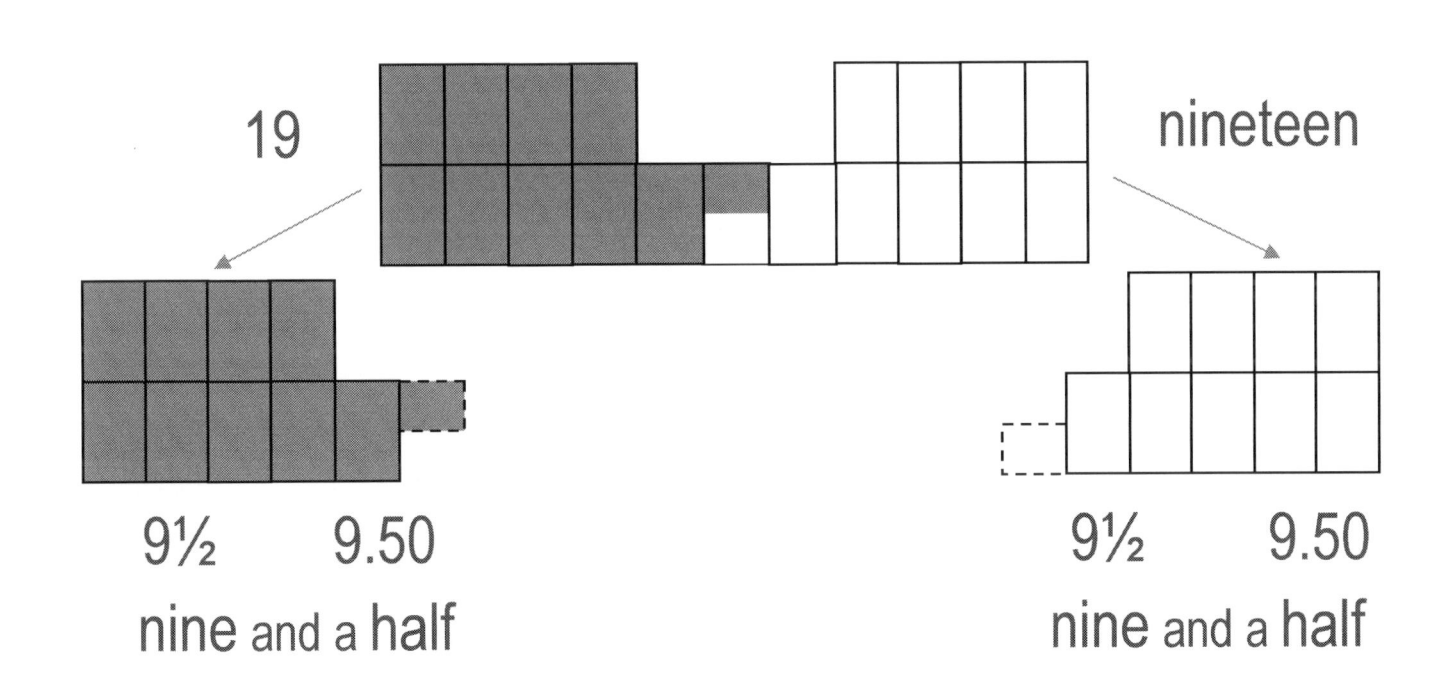

Sharing equally (2 people)

Divide by 2

÷2   x $\frac{1}{2}$ x ½

Ali

Asha

17

seventeen

8½   8.50

eight and a half

8½   8.50

eight and a half

19

nineteen

9½   9.50

nine and a half

9½   9.50

nine and a half

Quartering 4

Ali and **Asha** also share things with their friends **Alex** and **Ella**. For the following shapes, everyone gets a **quarter** (one-fourth) or **half** of **half**! That's **halving** for two groups. Then **halving** *again* for each.

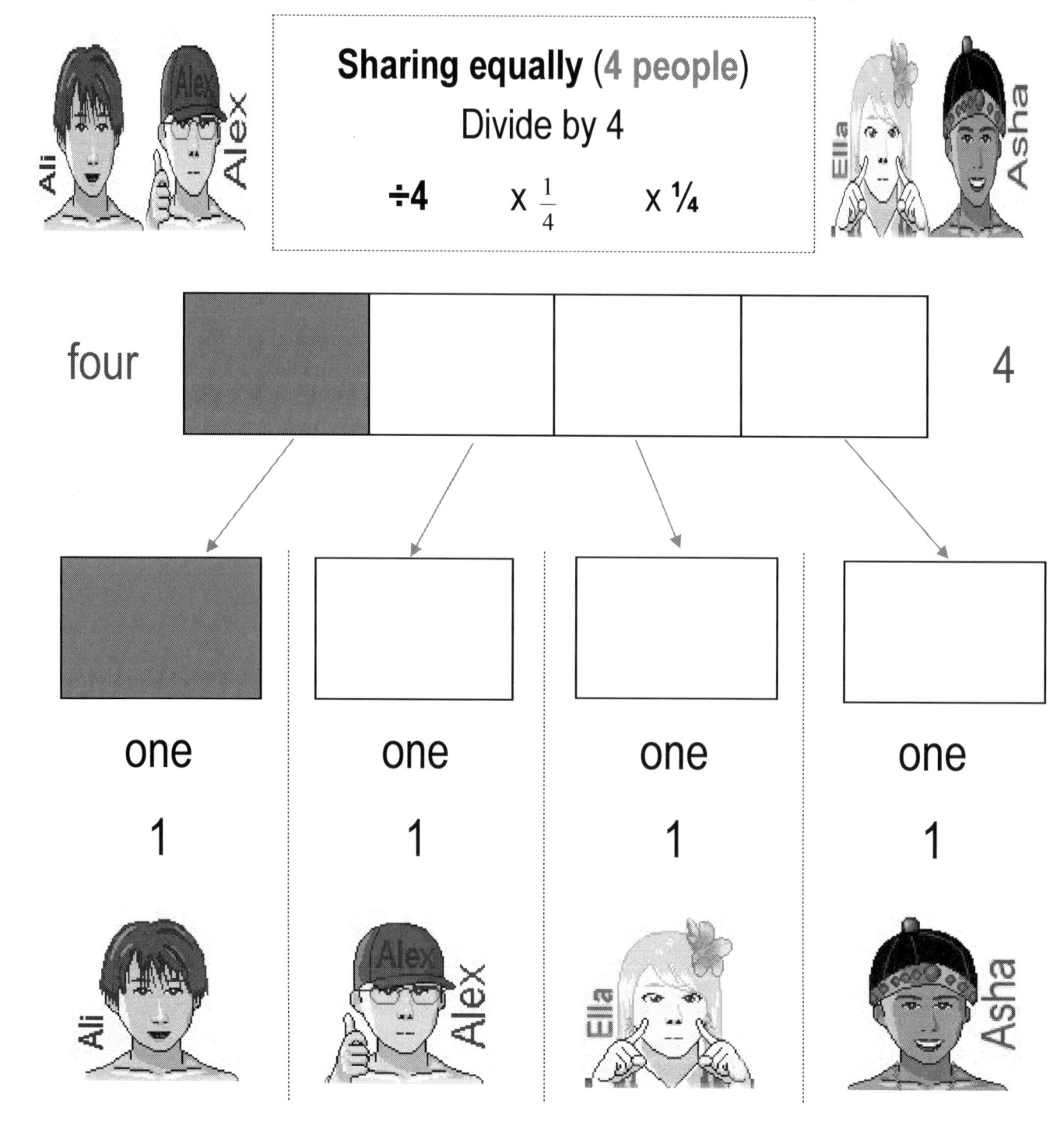

Sharing equally (4 people)
Divide by 4

$\div 4$ $\times \frac{1}{4}$ $\times ¼$

four   4

one   one   one   one
1   1   1   1

Quartering 8, 12

eight　8

Ali	Alex	Ella	Asha
two	two	two	two
2	2	2	2

twelve　12

Ali	Alex	Ella	Asha
three	three	three	three
3	3	3	3

Quartering 16, 20

sixteen　16

Ali　Alex　Ella　Asha

four　four　four　four
4　4　4　4

twenty　20

Ali　Alex　Ella　Asha

five　five　five　five
5　5　5　5

Quartering 2

Sharing equally (4 people)

Divide by 4

÷4   x $\frac{1}{4}$ x ¼

two

2

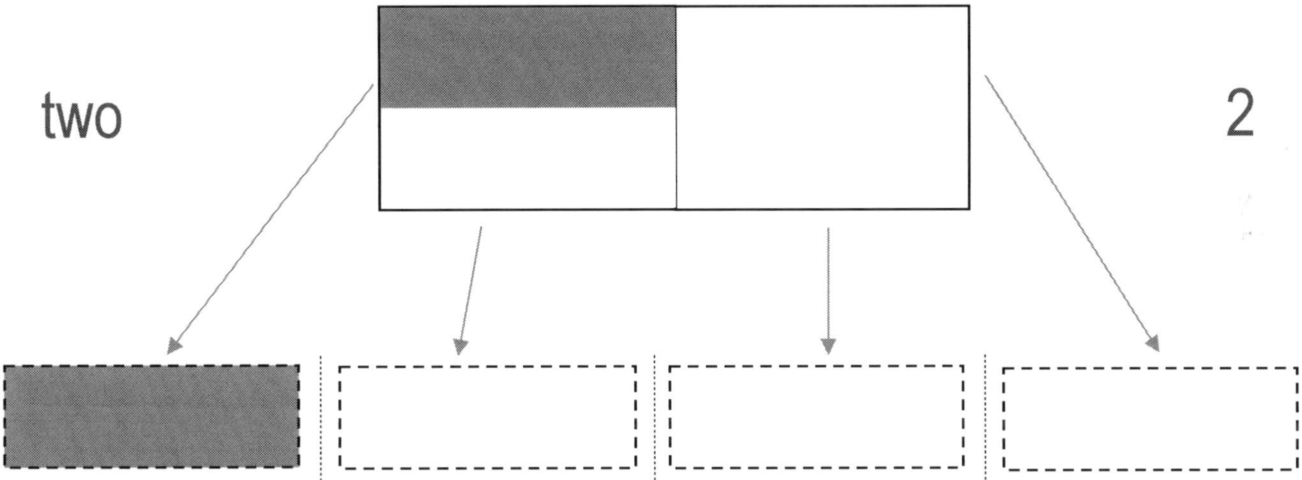

| half | half | half | half |

$\frac{1}{2}$ $\frac{1}{2}$ $\frac{1}{2}$ $\frac{1}{2}$

0.50   0.50   0.50   0.50

Quartering 6, 10

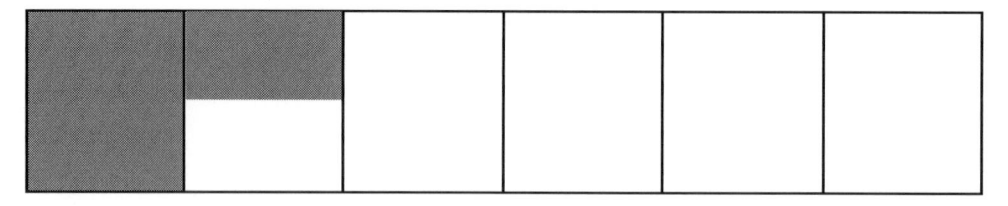

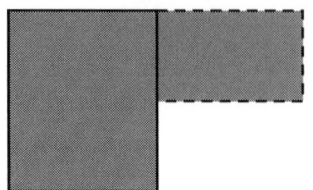

six   6

Ali | Alex | Ella | Asha

one and half | one and half | one and half | one and half

$1\frac{1}{2}$ 1.50 | $1\frac{1}{2}$ 1.50 | $1\frac{1}{2}$ 1.50 | $1\frac{1}{2}$ 1.50

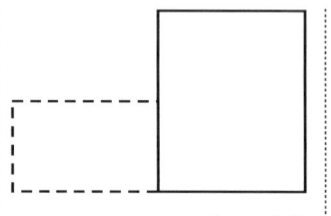

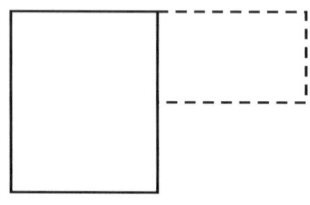

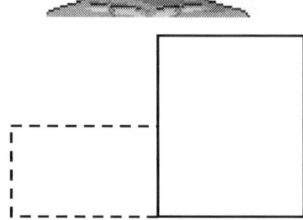

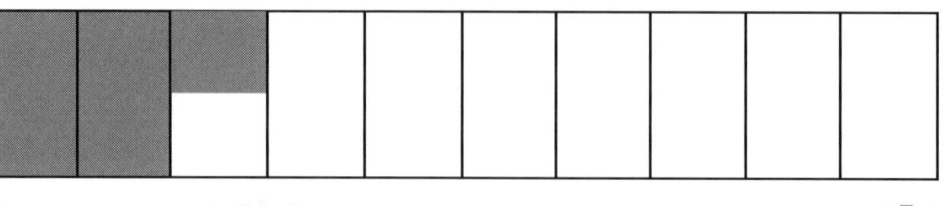

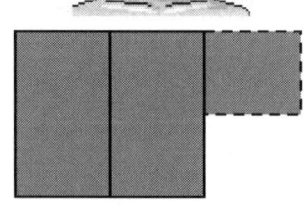

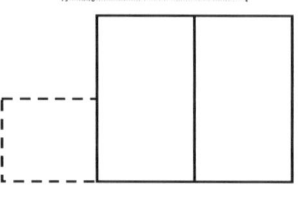

ten   10

Ali | Alex | Ella | Asha

two and half | two and half | two and half | two and half

$2\frac{1}{2}$ 2.50 | $2\frac{1}{2}$ 2.50 | $2\frac{1}{2}$ 2.50 | $2\frac{1}{2}$ 2.50

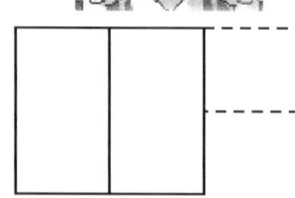

Quartering 14, 18

fourteen 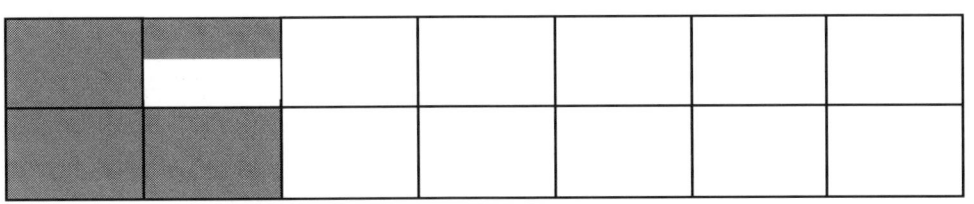   14

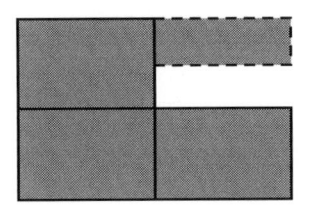

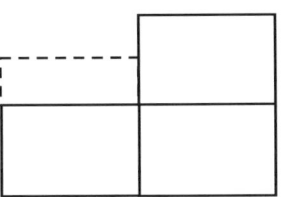

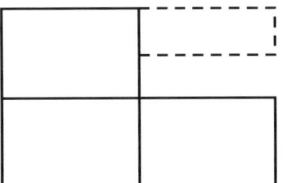

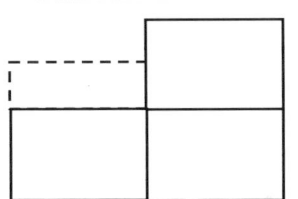

Ali	Alex	Ella	Asha
three and half	three and half	three and half	three and half
$3\frac{1}{2}$ 3.50	$3\frac{1}{2}$ 3.50	$3\frac{1}{2}$ 3.50	$3\frac{1}{2}$ 3.50

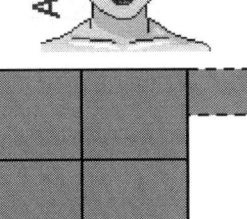

eighteen 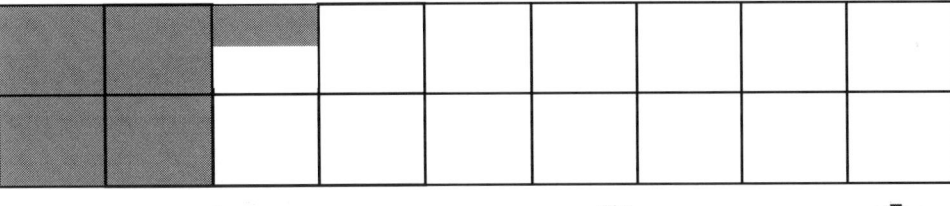   18

Ali	Alex	Ella	Asha
four and half	four and half	four and half	four and half
$4\frac{1}{2}$ 4.50	$4\frac{1}{2}$ 4.50	$4\frac{1}{2}$ 4.50	$4\frac{1}{2}$ 4.50

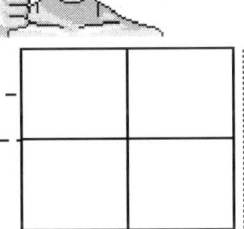

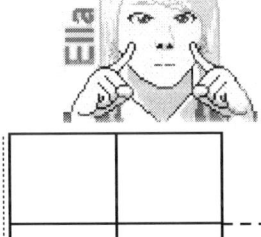

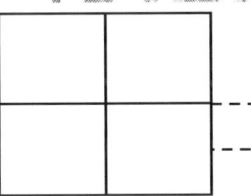

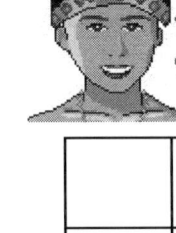

Quartering 1

Sharing equally (4 people)

Divide by 4

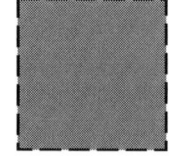

$\div 4$ $\times \frac{1}{4}$ $\times ¼$

one 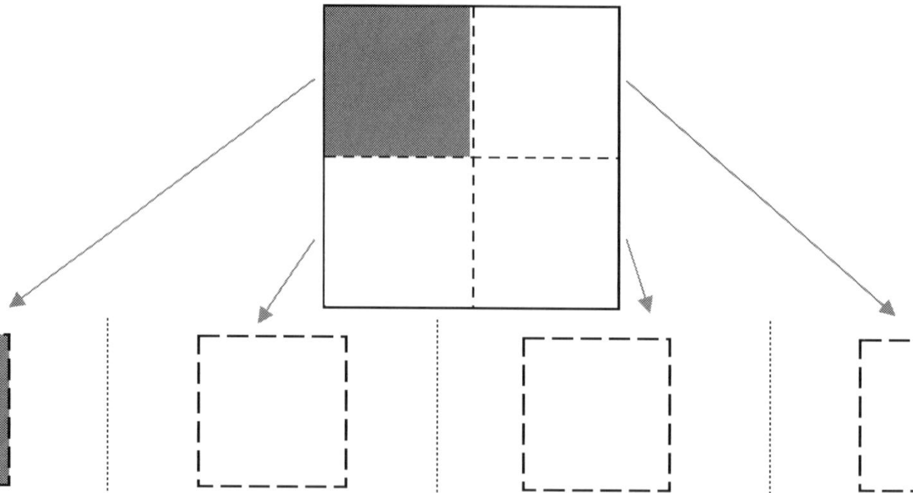 1

quarter	quarter	quarter	quarter
$\frac{1}{4}$	$\frac{1}{4}$	$\frac{1}{4}$	$\frac{1}{4}$
0.25	0.25	0.25	0.25

Quartering 5, 9

five 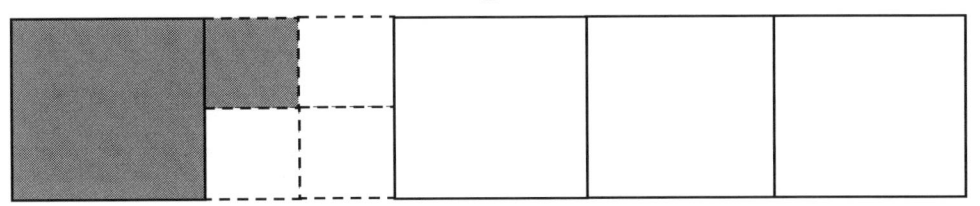　　　　　　　　　　　　　　　　　　　　　　5

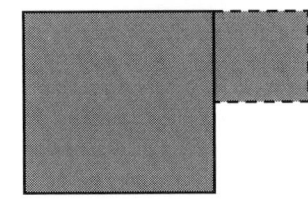

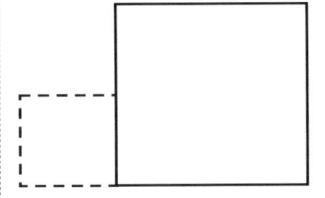

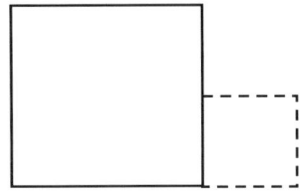

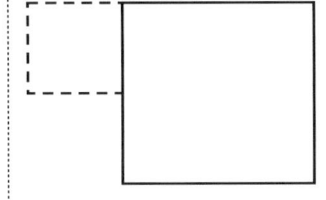

Ali	Alex	Ella	Asha
one and quarter	one and quarter	one and quarter	one and quarter
$1\frac{1}{4}$　1.25	$1\frac{1}{4}$　1.25	$1\frac{1}{4}$　1.25	$1\frac{1}{4}$　1.25

nine 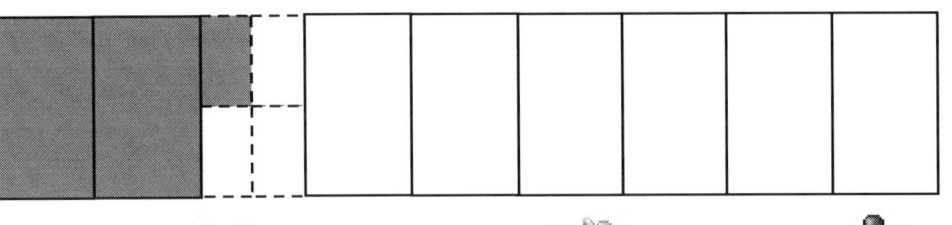　　　　　　　　　　　　　　　　　　　　　　9

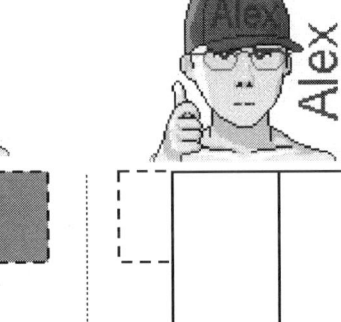

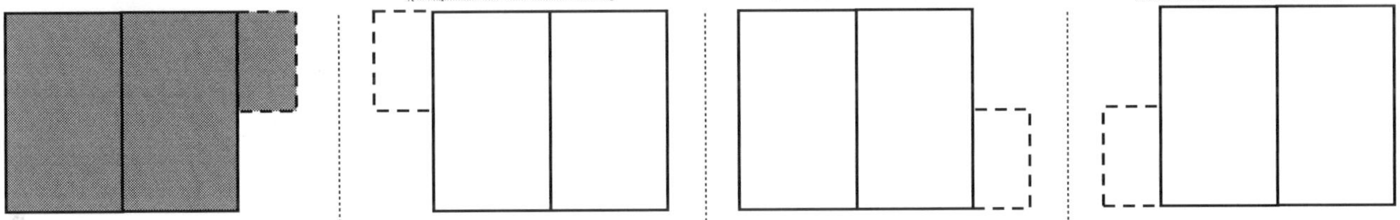

Ali	Alex	Ella	Asha
two and quarter	two and quarter	two and quarter	two and quarter
$2\frac{1}{4}$　2.25	$2\frac{1}{4}$　2.25	$2\frac{1}{4}$　2.25	$2\frac{1}{4}$　2.25

Quartering 13, 17

thirteen 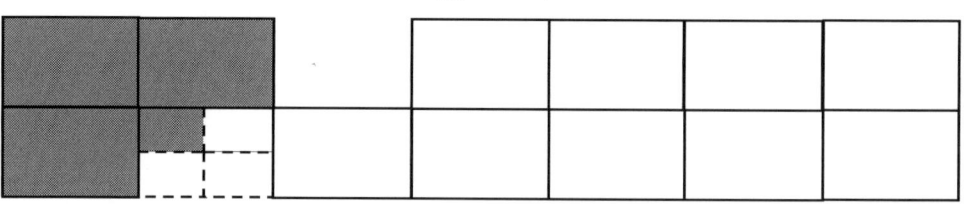   13

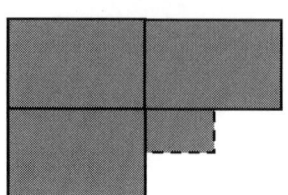

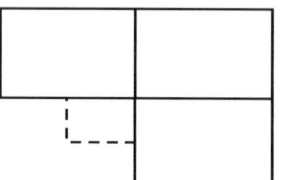

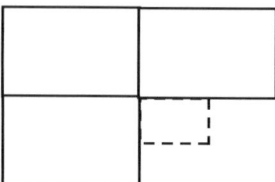

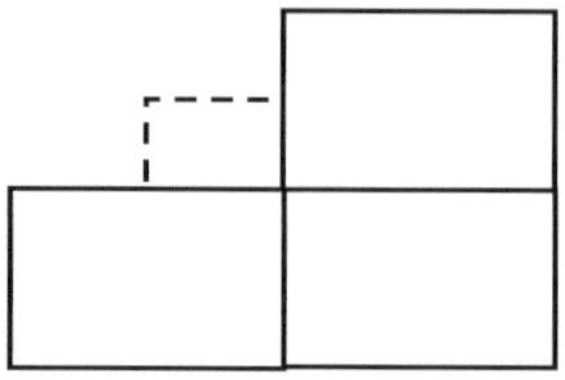

Ali | Alex | Ella | Asha

three and quarter | three and quarter | three and quarter | three and quarter

$3\frac{1}{4}$ 3.25 | $3\frac{1}{4}$ 3.25 | $3\frac{1}{4}$ 3.25 | $3\frac{1}{4}$ 3.25

seventeen 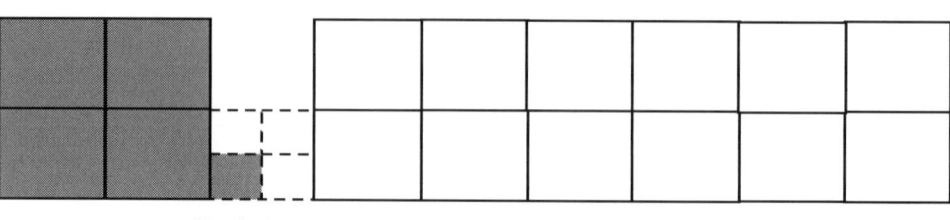   17

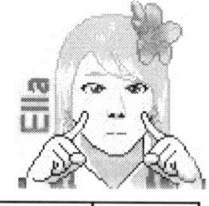

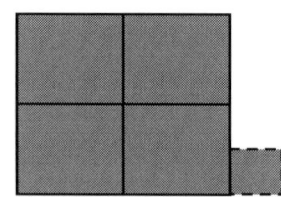

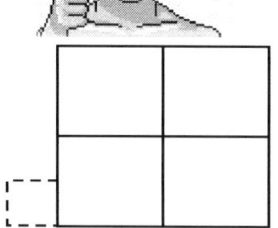

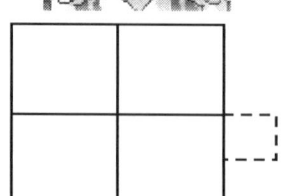

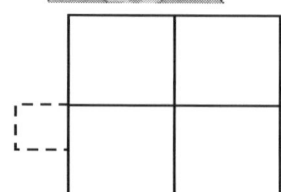

Ali | Alex | Ella | Asha

four and quarter | four and quarter | four and quarter | four and quarter

$4\frac{1}{4}$ 4.25 | $4\frac{1}{4}$ 4.25 | $4\frac{1}{4}$ 4.25 | $4\frac{1}{4}$ 4.25

Quartering 3

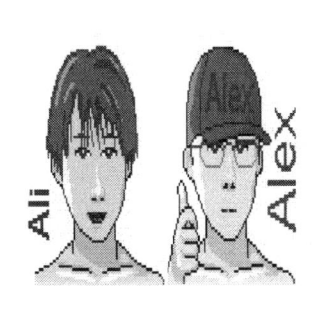

Sharing equally (4 people)

Divide by 4

÷4 $\times \dfrac{1}{4}$ × ¼

three 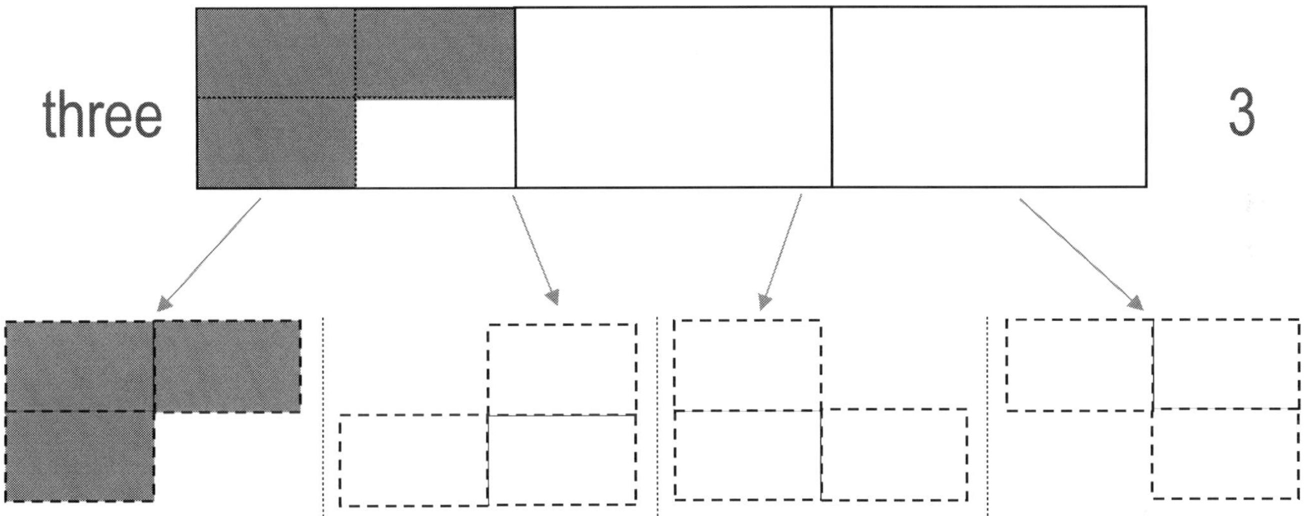   3

three-quarters | three-quarters | three-quarters | three-quarters

$\dfrac{3}{4}$ | $\dfrac{3}{4}$ | $\dfrac{3}{4}$ | $\dfrac{3}{4}$

0.75 | 0.75 | 0.75 | 0.75

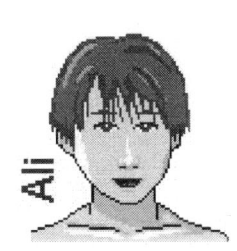

Quartering 7, 11

seven 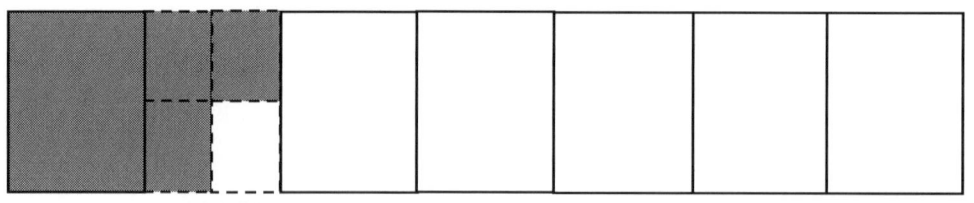   7

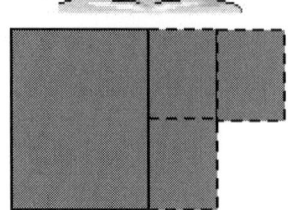

Ali
one and
three-quarters

$1\frac{3}{4}$ 1.75

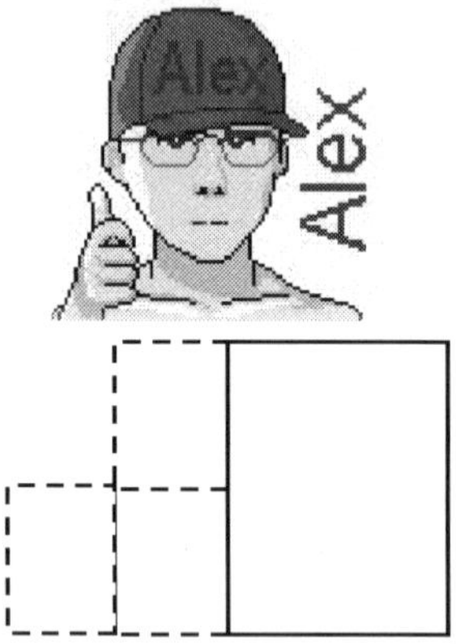

Alex
one and
three-quarters

$1\frac{3}{4}$ 1.75

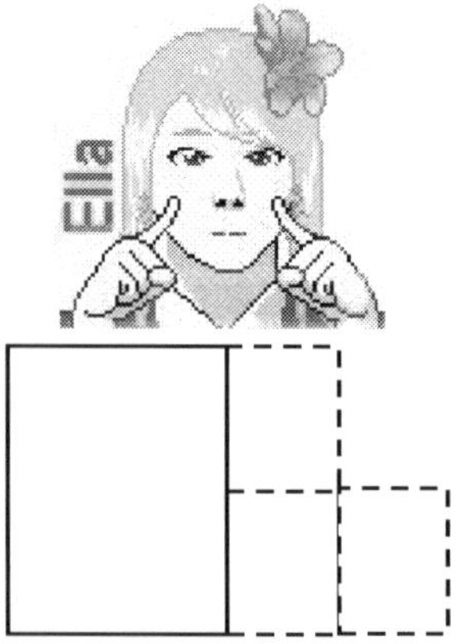

Ella
one and
three-quarters

$1\frac{3}{4}$ 1.75

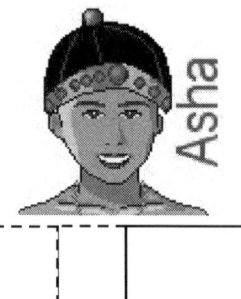

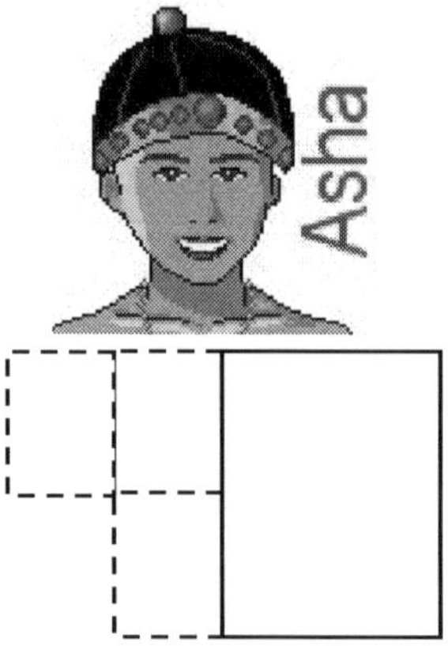

Asha
one and
three-quarters

$1\frac{3}{4}$ 1.75

eleven 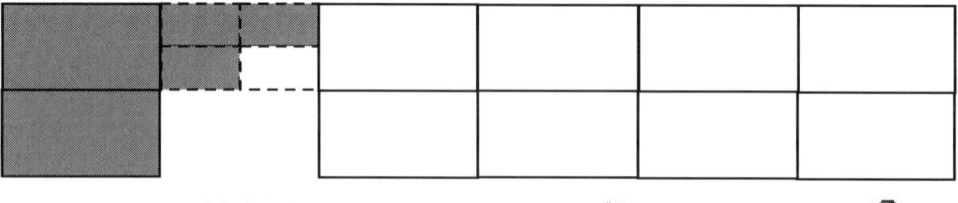   11

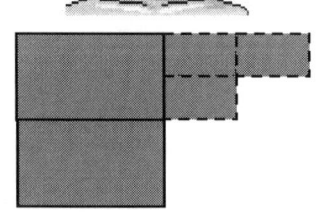

Ali
two and
three-quarters

$2\frac{3}{4}$ 2.75

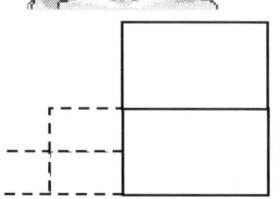

Alex
two and
three-quarters

$2\frac{3}{4}$ 2.75

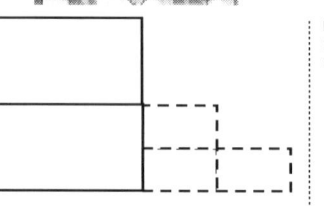

Ella
two and
three-quarters

$2\frac{3}{4}$ 2.75

Asha
two and
three-quarters

$2\frac{3}{4}$ 2.75

Quartering 15, 19

fifteen 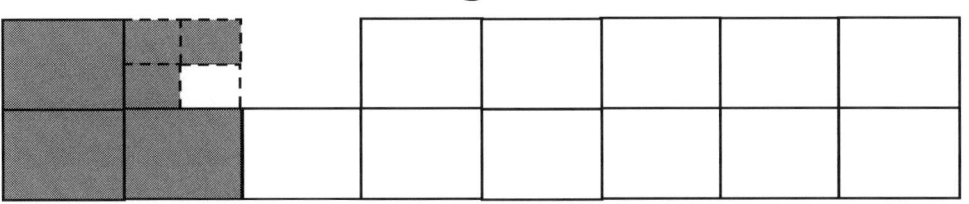　　　　　　　　　　　　　　　　　　　　　　　　　　15

Ali	Alex	Ella	Asha
three and three-quarters	three and three-quarters	three and three-quarters	three and three-quarters
$3\frac{3}{4}$　3.75	$3\frac{3}{4}$　3.75	$3\frac{3}{4}$　3.75	$3\frac{3}{4}$　3.75

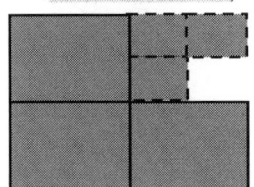

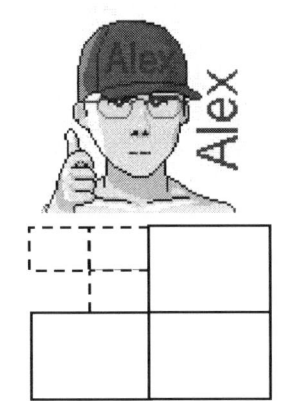

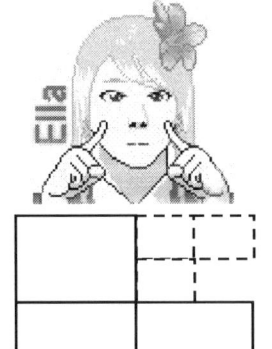

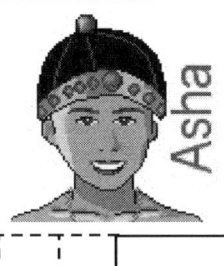

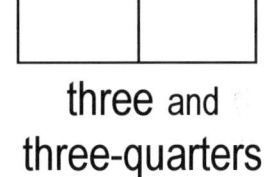

nineteen 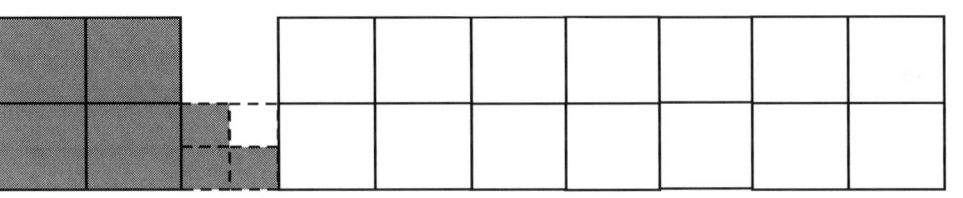　　　　　　　　　　　　　　　　　　　　　　　　19

Ali	Alex	Ella	Asha
four and three-quarters	four and three-quarters	four and three-quarters	four and three-quarters
$4\frac{3}{4}$　4.75	$4\frac{3}{4}$　4.75	$4\frac{3}{4}$　4.75	$4\frac{3}{4}$　4.75

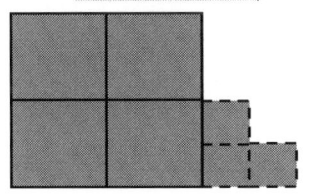

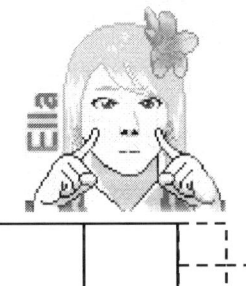

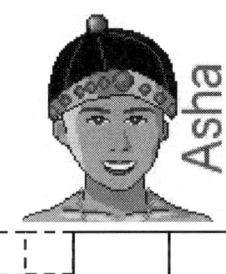

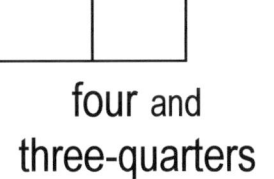

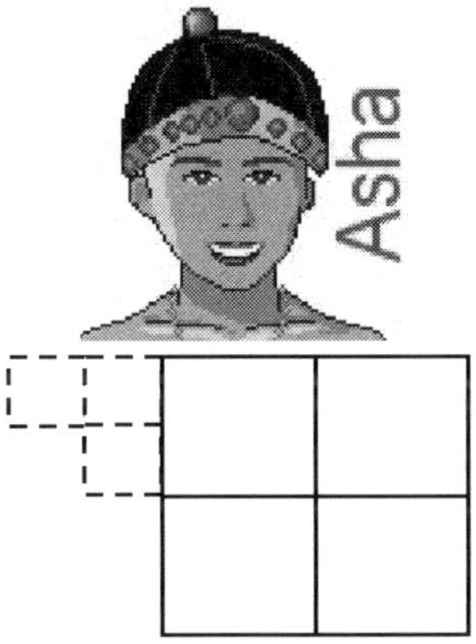

Equivalent Fractions

Equivalent means *equal in value*.

For example, if **2** children share **1** whole cake, they each get a **half**.

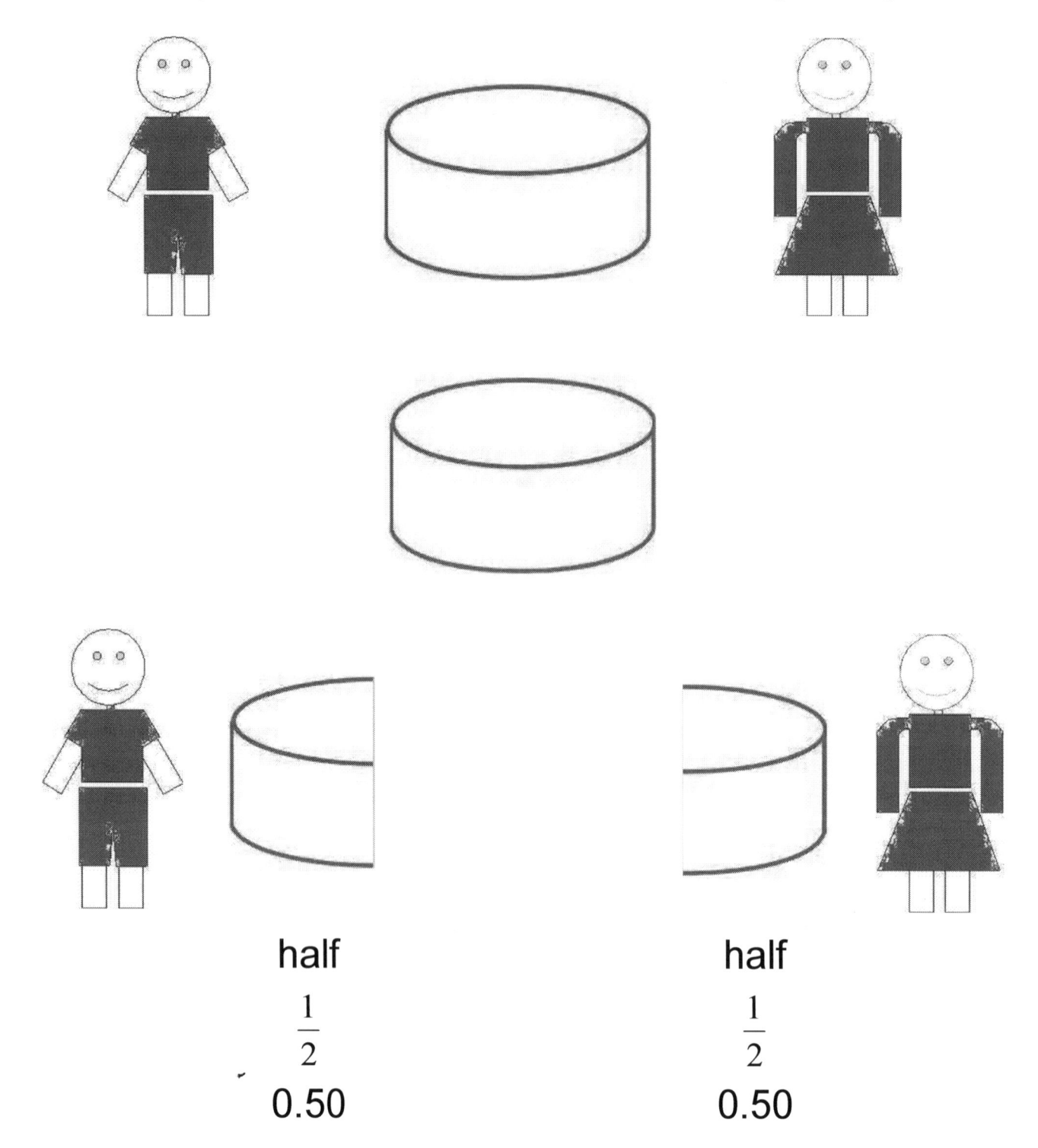

half
$\frac{1}{2}$
0.50

half
$\frac{1}{2}$
0.50

Also, if the same **two** children share **the same** whole **cake**, they can get **two-quarters** each. **Quarter** means **half of a half**.

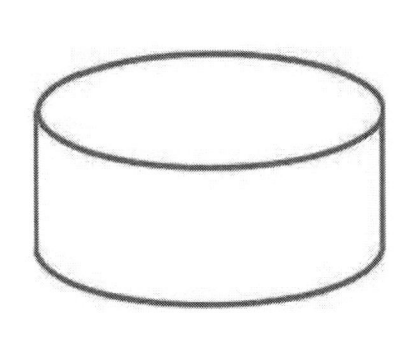

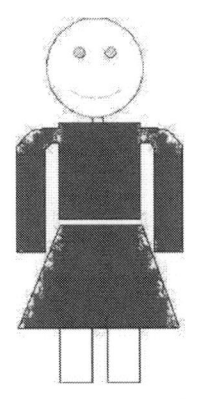

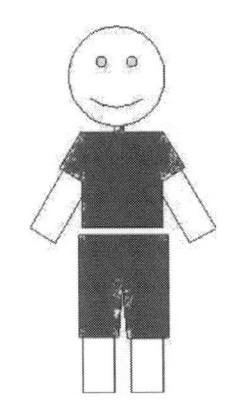

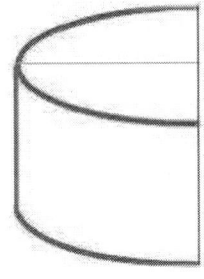

half
$\frac{1}{2}$
0.50

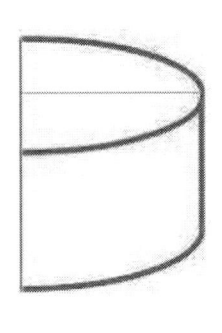

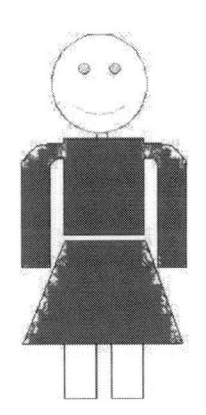

half
$\frac{1}{2}$
0.50

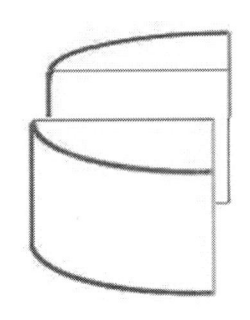

two-quarters
$\frac{2}{4}$
0.50

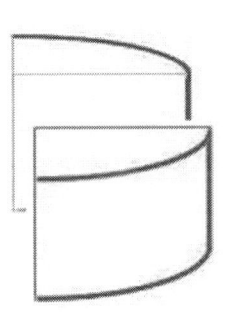

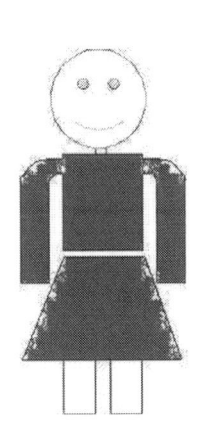

two-quarters
$\frac{2}{4}$
0.50

So, you can divide one whole cake into two halves (each child gets a half) or into four quarters (each child gets two-quarters).

Therefore, **half** is the same as **two-quarters**; both equal to **0.50**!

$$\frac{1}{2} = \frac{2}{4} = 0.50$$ or

Equivalent fractions are fractions with the **same value** even though their **numerators** and **denominators** may be **different**.

For example:

$$\frac{1}{2} \xrightarrow{\times 2} \frac{2}{4} \xrightarrow{\times 2} \frac{4}{8}$$

That is, if you **multiply** (or **divide**) both the numerator and the denominator of a fraction by the same non-zero number, **the value** of that fraction **always stays the same**!
The fraction only changes into a different equivalent fraction.

This is because multiplying the top and the bottom of a fraction by the same non-zero number is the same as multiplying that fraction by one!

This is the principle of **equivalent fractions**.

$$\frac{1}{2} \xrightarrow{\times 2} \frac{2}{4} \quad \text{or} \quad \square \times \frac{2}{2} (=\times 1) = \square$$

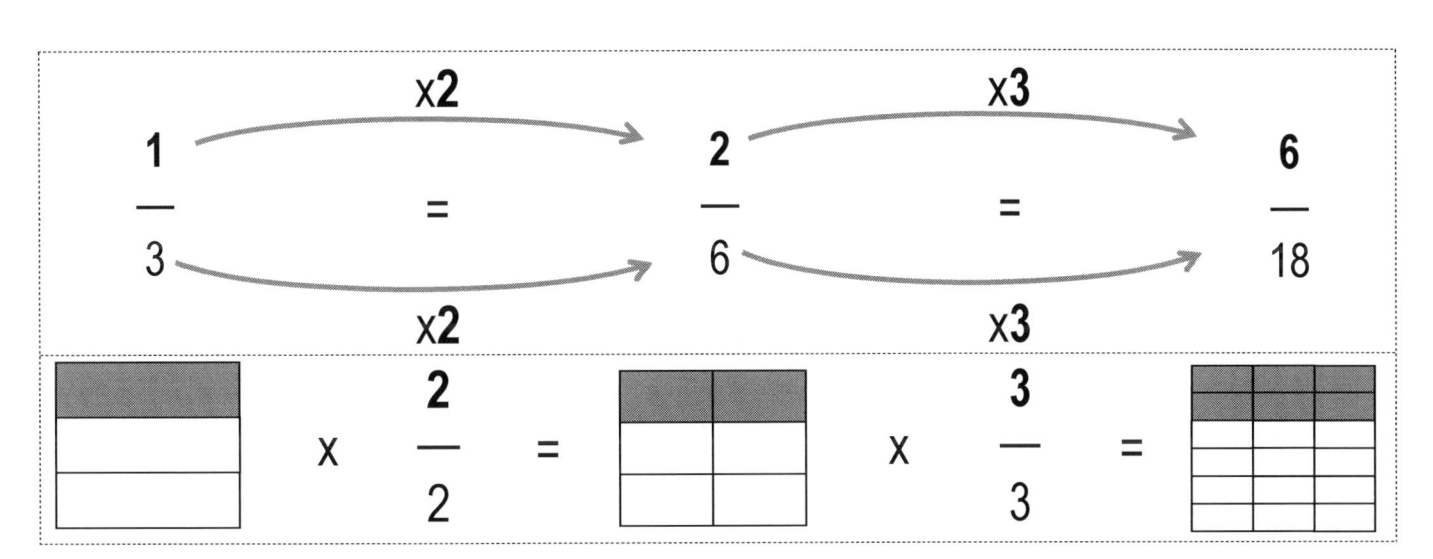

$$\frac{1}{2} \xrightarrow{\times 5} \frac{5}{10} \quad \text{or} \quad \square \times \frac{5}{5} (=\times 1) = \square$$

$$\frac{1}{5} \xrightarrow{\times 2} \frac{2}{10} \quad \text{or} \quad \square \times \frac{2}{2} (=\times 1) = \square$$

$$\frac{1}{3} \xrightarrow{\times 2} \frac{2}{6} \xrightarrow{\times 3} \frac{6}{18}$$

$$\square \times \frac{2}{2} = \square \times \frac{3}{3} = \square$$

And so on.

Halves

| Fraction | → | Equivalent Fraction | → | Decimal |

$\dfrac{0}{2}$ = $\dfrac{0}{1}$ = 0 = **0.00**

nothing   nothing

$\dfrac{1}{2}$ = **0.50**

half

$\dfrac{2}{2}$ = $\dfrac{1}{1}$ = 1 = **1.00**

two-halves   one, whole

1) Quarters

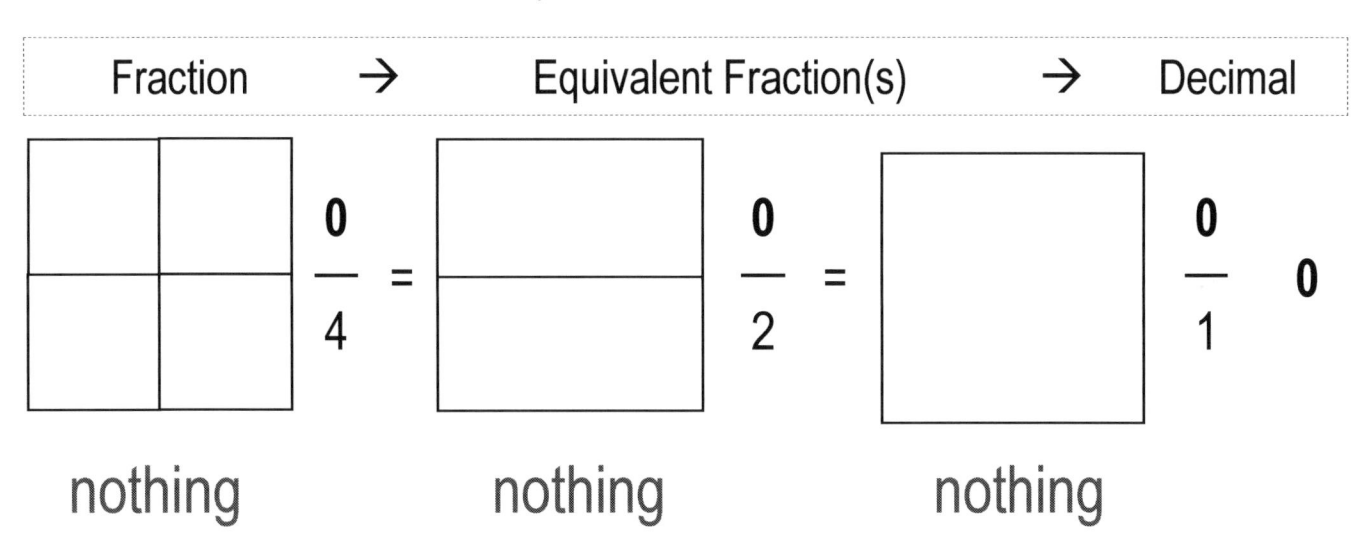

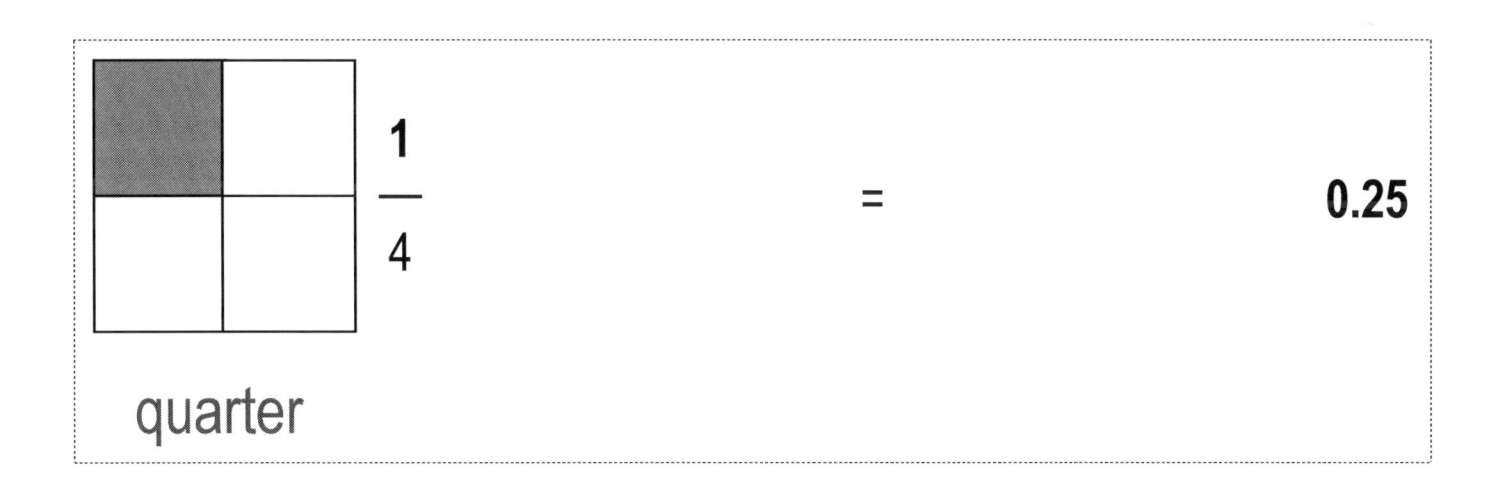

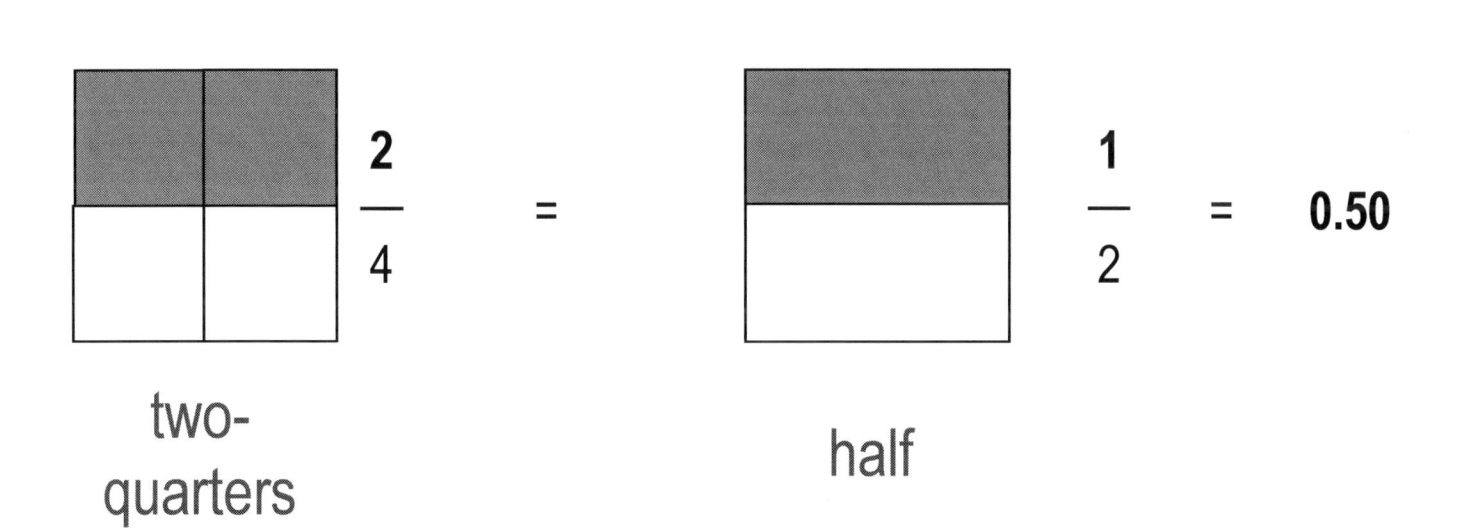

| Fraction | → | Equivalent Fraction(s) | → | Decimal |

$$\frac{0}{4} = \frac{0}{2} = \frac{0}{1} \quad 0$$

nothing — nothing — nothing

$$\frac{1}{4} = 0.25$$

quarter

$$\frac{2}{4} = \frac{1}{2} = 0.50$$

two-quarters — half

2) **Quarters**

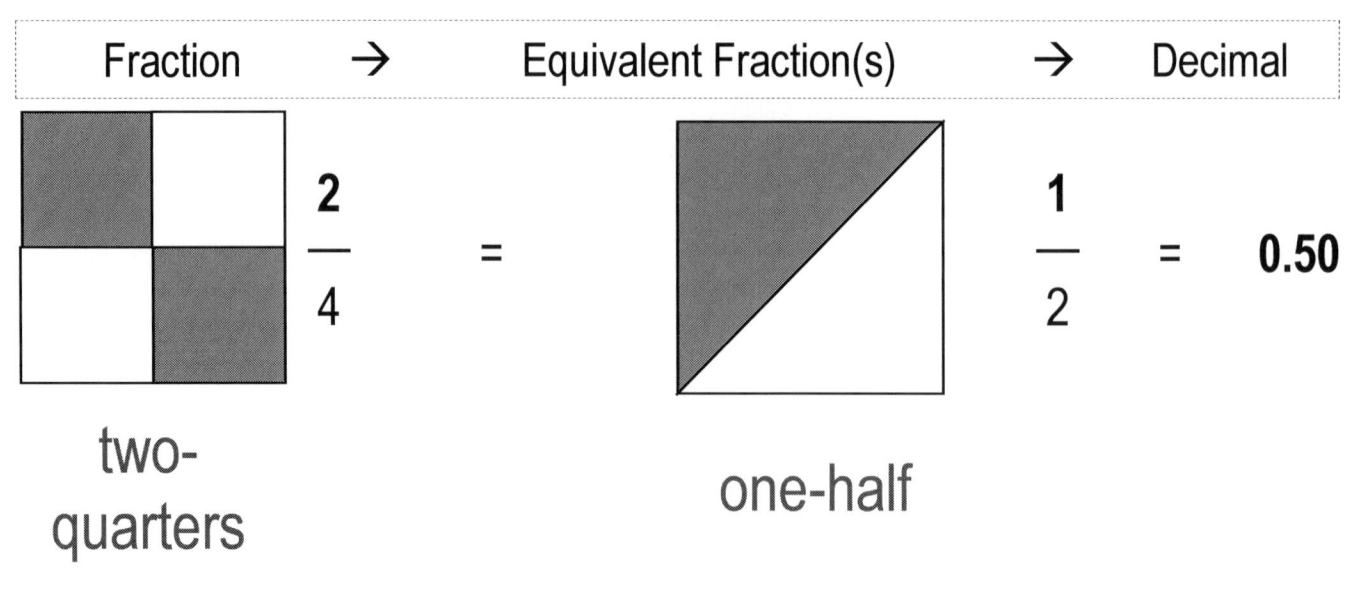

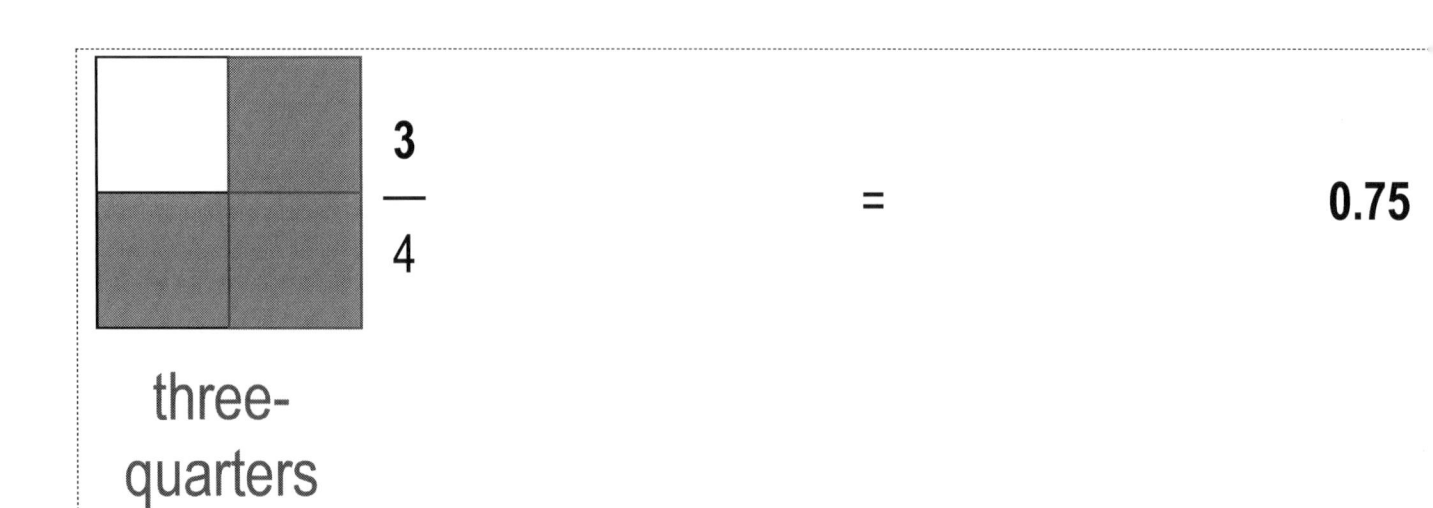

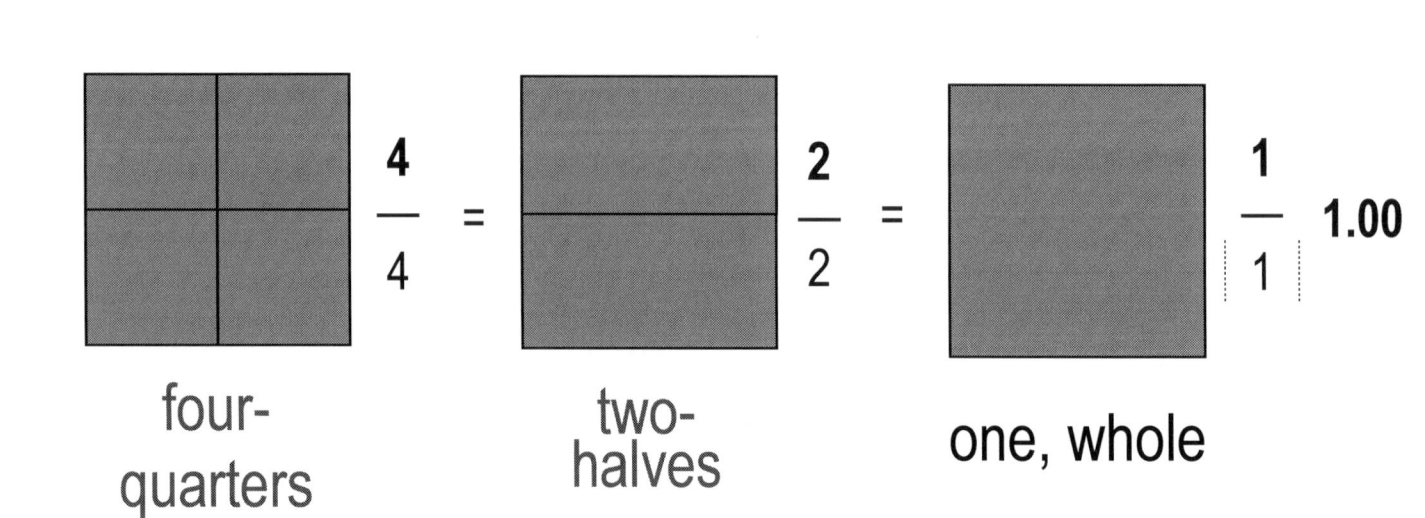

| Fraction | → | Equivalent Fraction(s) | → | Decimal |

$\dfrac{2}{4}$ = $\dfrac{1}{2}$ = **0.50**

two-quarters

one-half

$\dfrac{3}{4}$ = **0.75**

three-quarters

$\dfrac{4}{4}$ = $\dfrac{2}{2}$ = $\dfrac{1}{1}$ **1.00**

four-quarters

two-halves

one, whole

Halves v Quarters

Fraction	Shape	Fraction Name Decimal	→	Fraction Name Decimal	Shape	Fraction
$\dfrac{0}{2}$		nothing 0	=	nothing 0		$\dfrac{0}{4}$
				quarter 0.25		$\dfrac{1}{4}$
$\dfrac{1}{2}$		half 0.50	=	two-quarters 0.50		$\dfrac{2}{4}$
				three-quarters 0.75		$\dfrac{3}{4}$
$\dfrac{2}{2}$		two-halves, one, whole 1.00	=	four-quarters, one, whole 1.00		$\dfrac{4}{4}$

1) Eighths

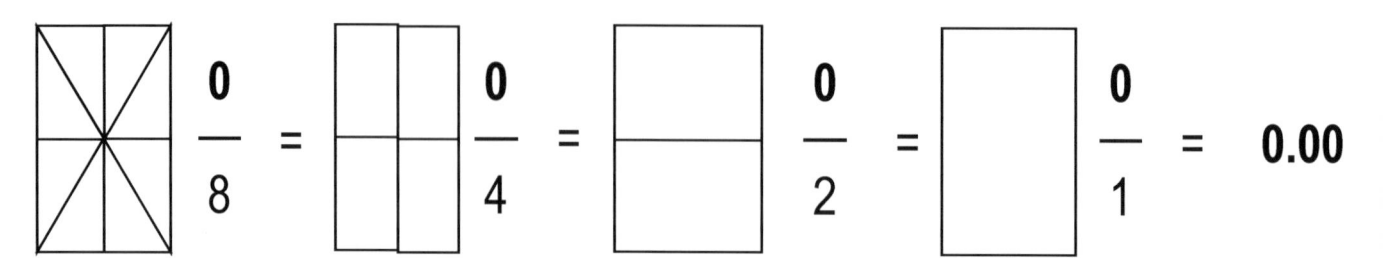

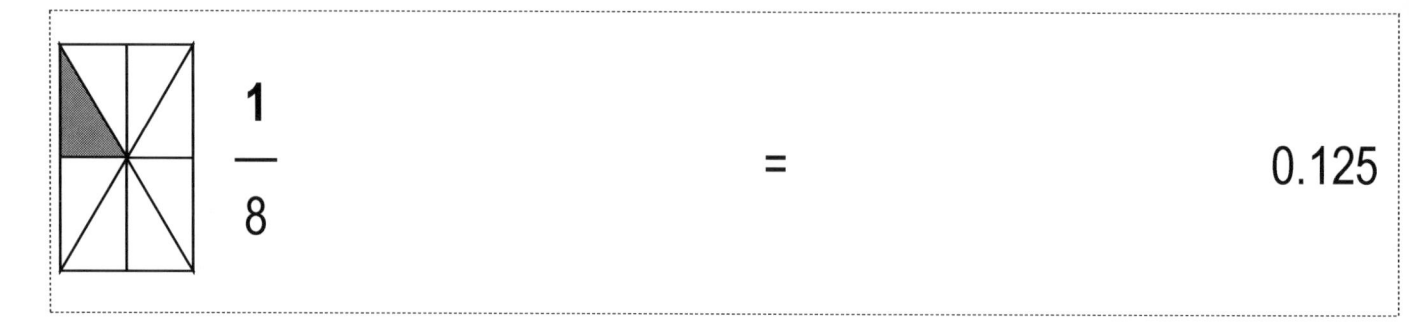

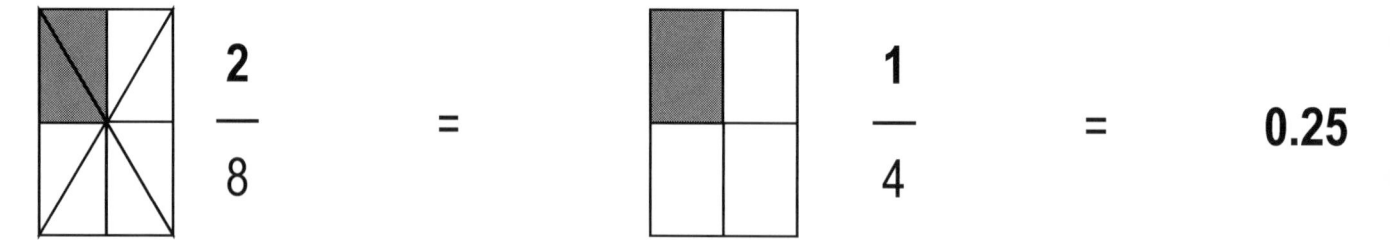

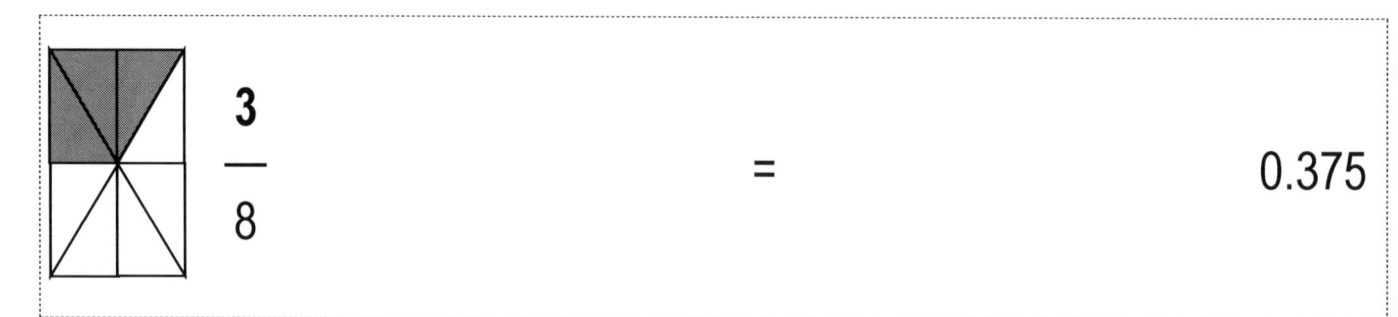

| Shape Fraction | → | Shape Fraction | → | Shape Fraction | → | Shape Fraction | Decimal |

$\dfrac{0}{8}$ = $\dfrac{0}{4}$ = $\dfrac{0}{2}$ = $\dfrac{0}{1}$ = **0.00**

$\dfrac{1}{8}$ = 0.125

$\dfrac{2}{8}$ = $\dfrac{1}{4}$ = **0.25**

$\dfrac{3}{8}$ = 0.375

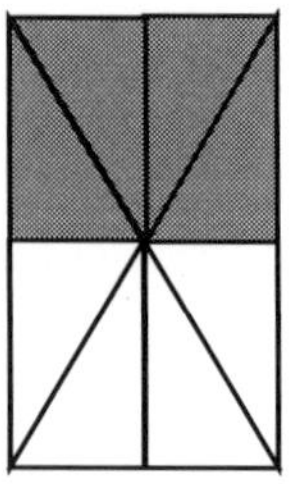

$\dfrac{4}{8}$ = $\dfrac{2}{4}$ = $\dfrac{1}{2}$ = **0.50**

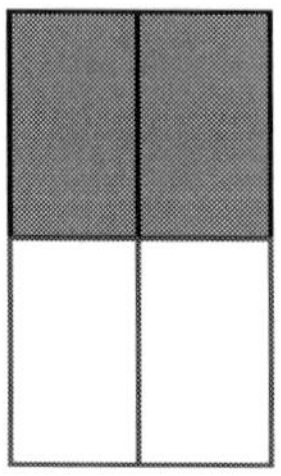

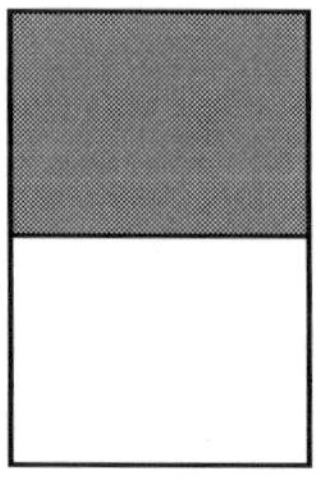

2) # Eighths

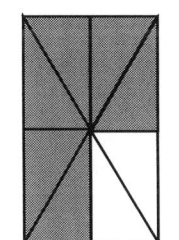

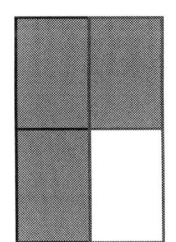

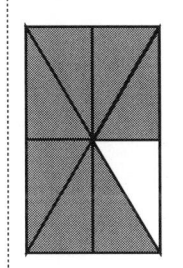

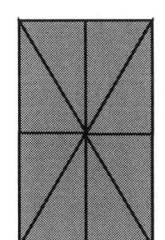

| Shape Fraction | → | Shape Fraction | → | Shape Fraction | Decimal |

$\dfrac{4}{8}$ = $\dfrac{2}{4}$ = $\dfrac{1}{2}$ = **0.50**

$\dfrac{5}{8}$ = 0.625

$\dfrac{6}{8}$ = $\dfrac{3}{4}$ = **0.75**

$\dfrac{7}{8}$ = 0.875

$\dfrac{8}{8}$ = $\dfrac{4}{4}$ = $\dfrac{2}{2}$ = $\dfrac{1}{1}$ = 1.00

I) # Quarters v Eighths

Fraction	Shape	Fraction Name / Decimal	→	Fraction Name / Decimal	Shape	Fraction
$\dfrac{0}{4}$		nothing 0	=	nothing 0		$\dfrac{0}{8}$
				one-eighth 0.125		$\dfrac{1}{8}$
$\dfrac{1}{4}$		quarter 0.25	=	two-eighths 0.25		$\dfrac{2}{8}$
				three-eighths 0.375		$\dfrac{3}{8}$
$\dfrac{2}{4}$		two-quarters 0.50	=	four-eighths 0.50		$\dfrac{4}{8}$

II) Quarters v Eighths

Fraction	Shape	Fraction Name Decimal	→	Fraction Name Decimal	Shape	Fraction
$\frac{2}{4}$		two-quarters 0.50	=	four-eighths 0.50		$\frac{4}{8}$
				five-eighths 0.625		$\frac{5}{8}$
$\frac{3}{4}$		three-quarters 0.75	=	six-eighths 0.75		$\frac{6}{8}$
				seven-eighths 0.875		$\frac{7}{8}$
$\frac{4}{4}$		four-quarters, one, whole 1.00	=	eight-eighths, one, whole 1.00		$\frac{8}{8}$

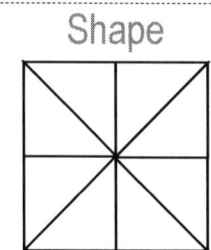

a) Halves v Quarters v Eighths

Fraction →	Fraction →	Fraction	Decimal
$\dfrac{0}{2}$ =	$\dfrac{0}{4}$ =	$\dfrac{0}{8}$ =	**0.00**
		$\dfrac{1}{8}$ =	0.125
	$\dfrac{1}{4}$ =	$\dfrac{2}{8}$ =	**0.25**
		$\dfrac{3}{8}$ =	0.375
$\dfrac{1}{2}$ =	$\dfrac{2}{4}$ =	$\dfrac{4}{8}$ =	**0.50**

b) # Halves v Quarters v Eighths

Fraction →	Fraction →	Fraction	Decimal

$\dfrac{1}{2}$ = $\dfrac{2}{4}$ = $\dfrac{4}{8}$ = **0.50**

$\dfrac{5}{8}$ = 0.625

$\dfrac{3}{4}$ = $\dfrac{6}{8}$ = **0.75**

$\dfrac{7}{8}$ = 0.875

$\dfrac{2}{2}$ = $\dfrac{4}{4}$ = $\dfrac{8}{8}$ = **1.00**

1) **Fifths**

Shape Fraction	→	Shape Fraction	→	Decimal

$\dfrac{0}{5}$ = $\dfrac{0}{1}$ = 0 = **0.00**

$\dfrac{1}{5}$ = 0.20

$\dfrac{2}{5}$ = 0.40

$\dfrac{2}{5}$ = 0.40

2) **Fifths**

| Shape Fraction | → | Shape | Fraction | → | Decimal |

$\dfrac{3}{5}$ = 0.60

$\dfrac{3}{5}$ = 0.60

$\dfrac{4}{5}$ = 0.80

$\dfrac{5}{5}$ = $\dfrac{1}{1}$ = 1 = 1.00

1) # Tenths

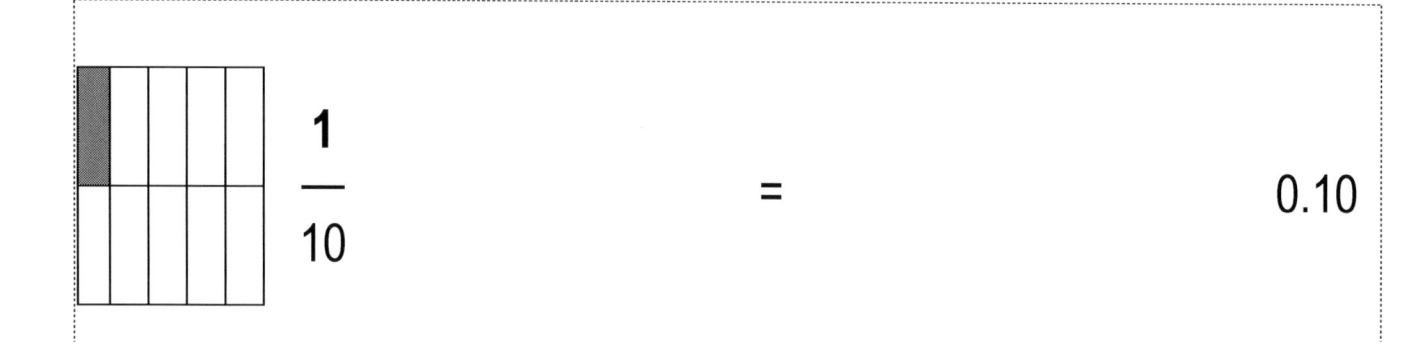

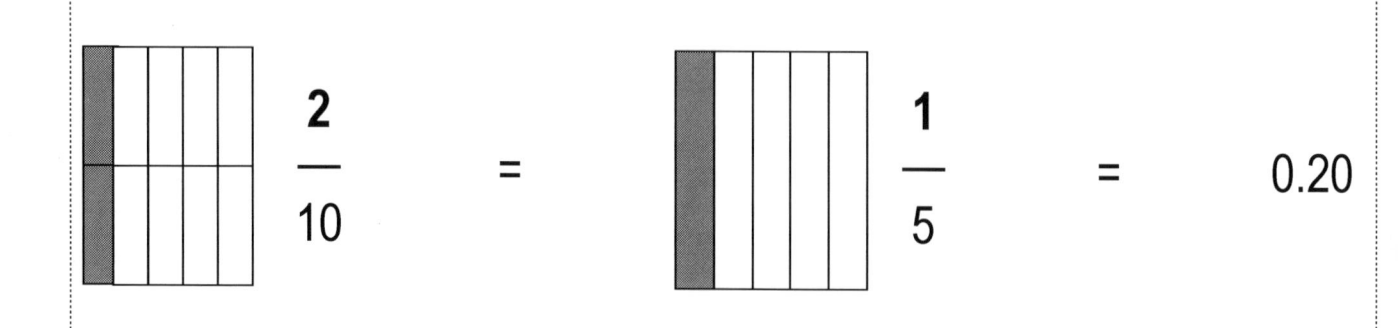

Fraction → Equivalent Fraction(s) → Decimal

$\dfrac{0}{10} = \dfrac{0}{5} = \dfrac{0}{1} = 0 = 0.00$

$\dfrac{1}{10} = 0.10$

$\dfrac{2}{10} = \dfrac{1}{5} = 0.20$

$\dfrac{3}{10} = 0.30$

II) **Tenths**

Fraction →	Equivalent Fraction →	Decimal
Shape	Equivalent Shape	

$\dfrac{4}{10}$ = $\dfrac{2}{5}$ = 0.40

$\dfrac{5}{10}$ = **0.50**

$\dfrac{6}{10}$ = $\dfrac{3}{5}$ = 0.60

III) **Tenths**

Fraction	→	Equivalent Fraction	→	Decimal

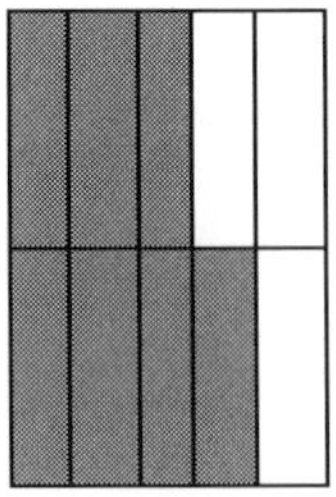

$\dfrac{7}{10}$ = = 0.70

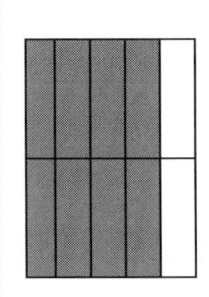

$\dfrac{8}{10}$ 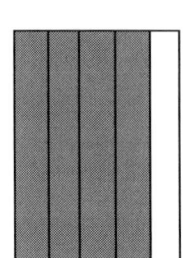 = $\dfrac{4}{5}$ = 0.80

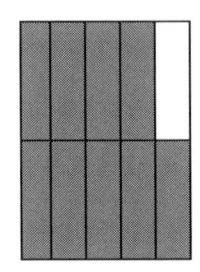

$\dfrac{9}{10}$ = 0.90

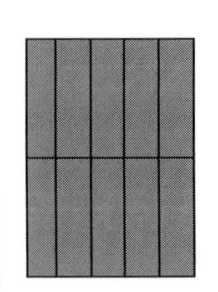

$\dfrac{10}{10}$ 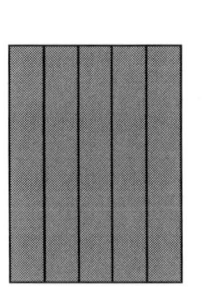 = $\dfrac{5}{5}$ = $\dfrac{1}{1}$ = 1.00

48

Quiz 1

> ➤ Find the **odd one** out?

Which of the following shapes is **not** a **fraction** (*tick*)?

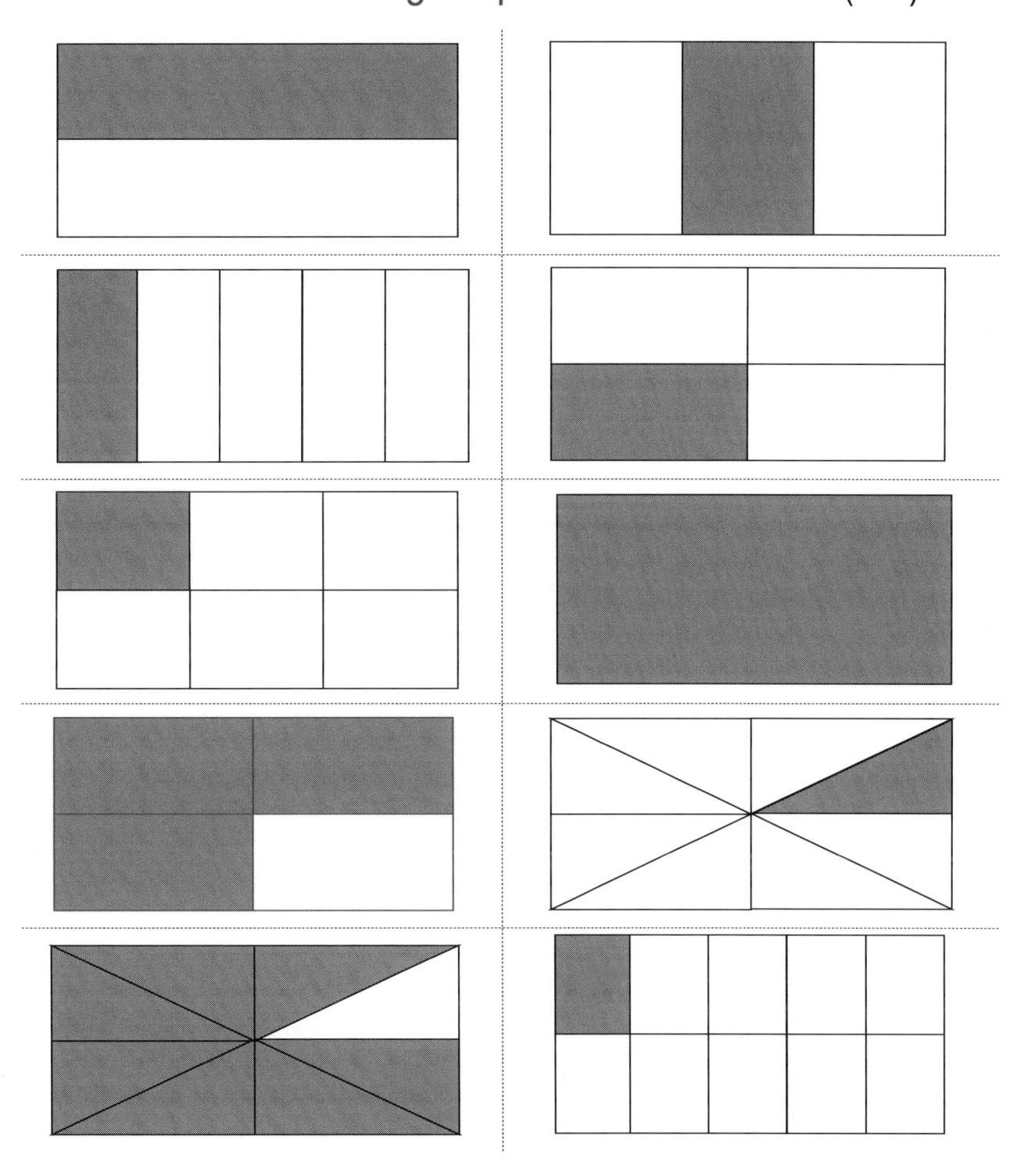

49

a) Fifths v Tenths

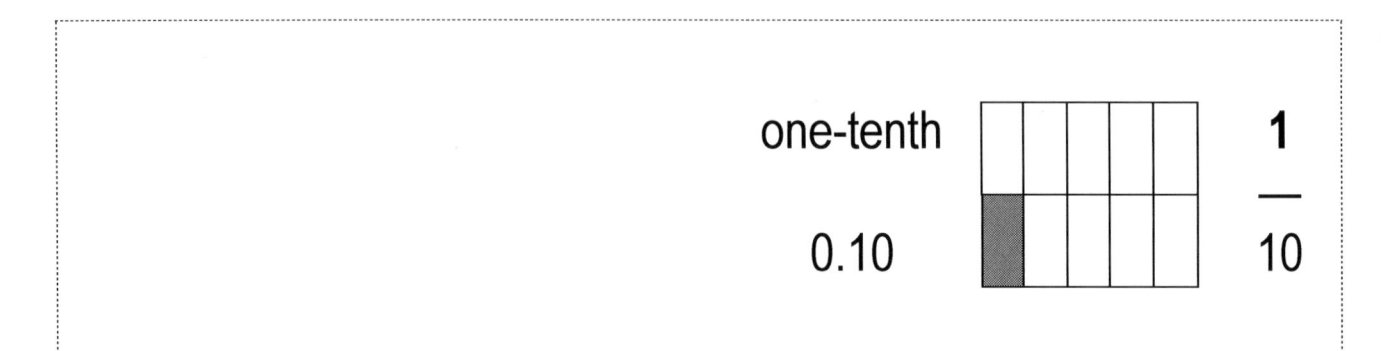

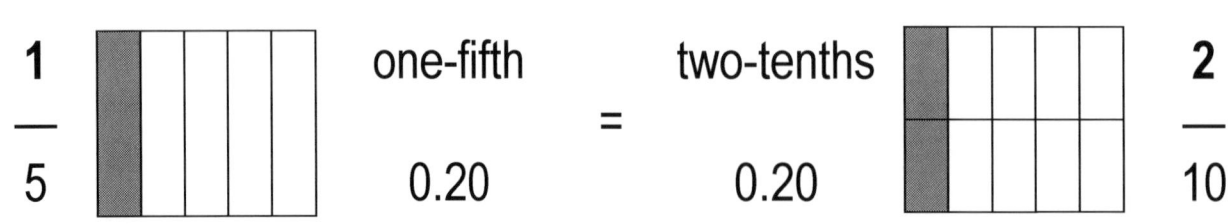

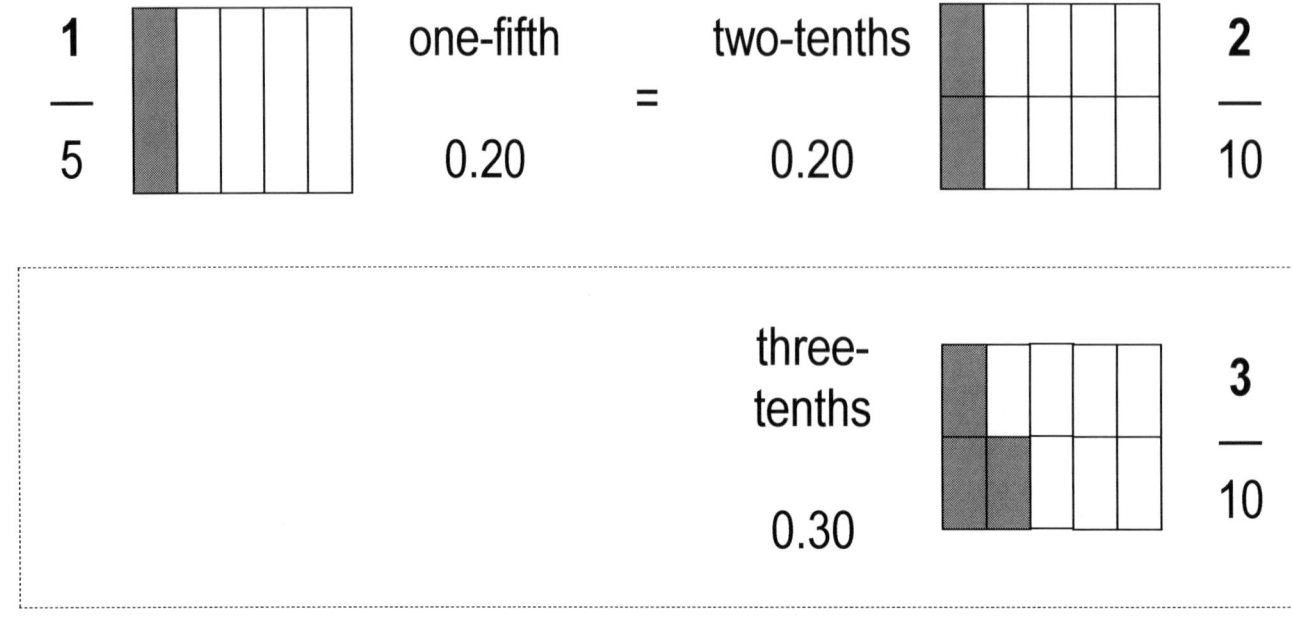

Fraction	Shape	Fraction Name / Decimal	→	Fraction Name / Decimal	Shape	Fraction

$\dfrac{0}{5}$ — nothing, 0 = nothing, 0 — $\dfrac{0}{10}$

one-tenth, 0.10 — $\dfrac{1}{10}$

$\dfrac{1}{5}$ — one-fifth, 0.20 = two-tenths, 0.20 — $\dfrac{2}{10}$

three-tenths, 0.30 — $\dfrac{3}{10}$

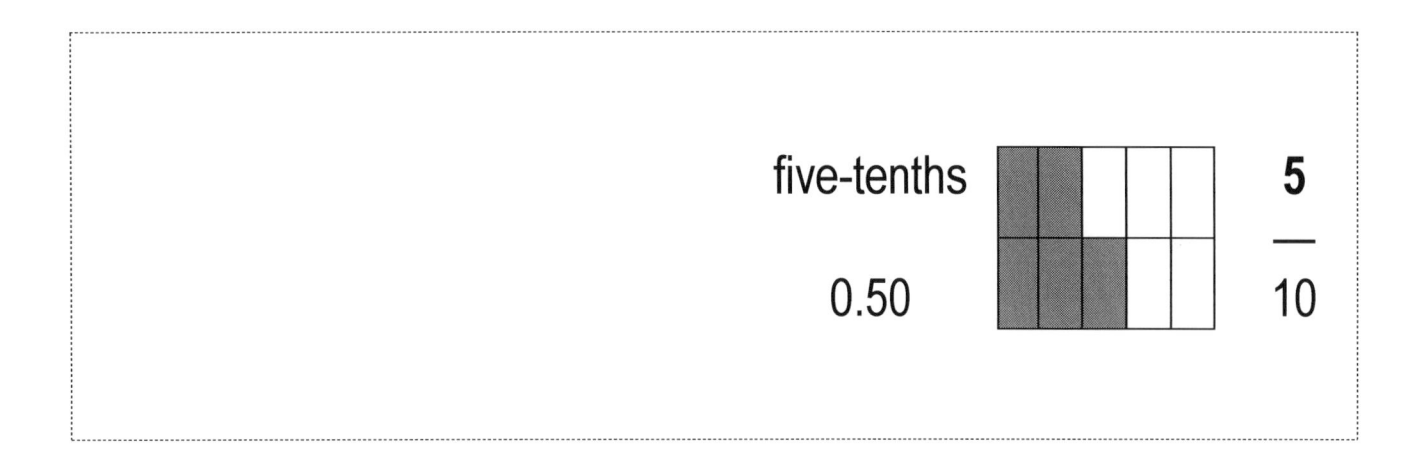

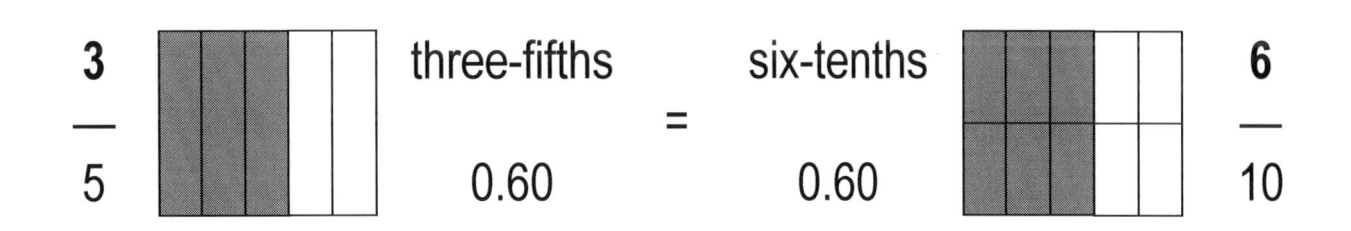

b) **Fifths v Tenths**

Fraction	Shape	Fraction Name / Decimal	→	Fraction Name / Decimal	Shape	Fraction

$\dfrac{2}{5}$ — two-fifths 0.40 = four-tenths 0.40 — $\dfrac{4}{10}$

five-tenths 0.50 — $\dfrac{5}{10}$

$\dfrac{3}{5}$ — three-fifths 0.60 = six-tenths 0.60 — $\dfrac{6}{10}$

51

c) **Fifths v Tenths**

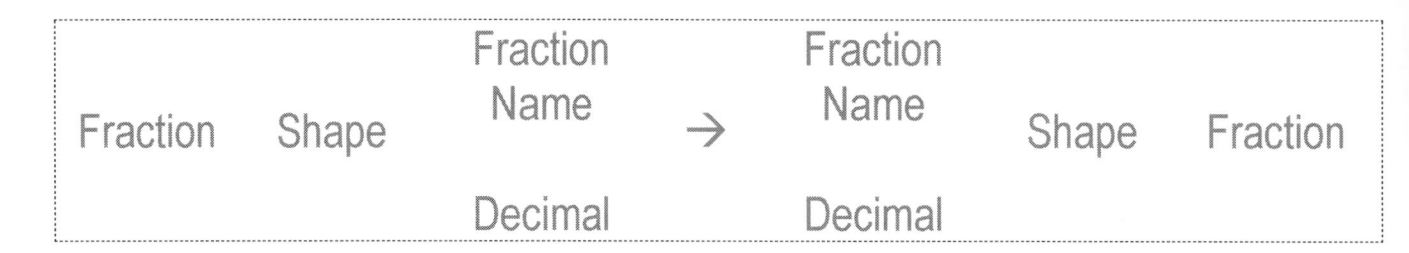

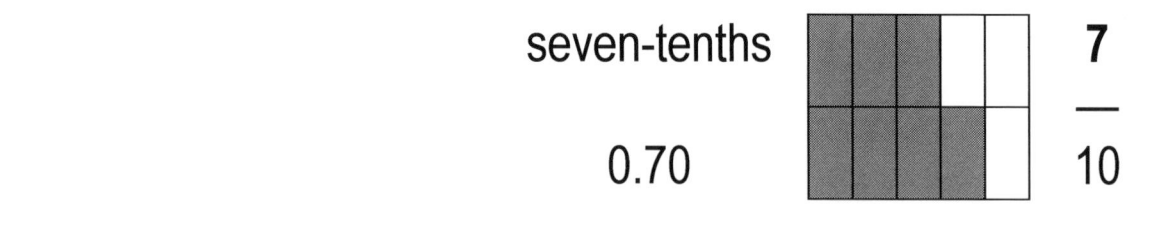

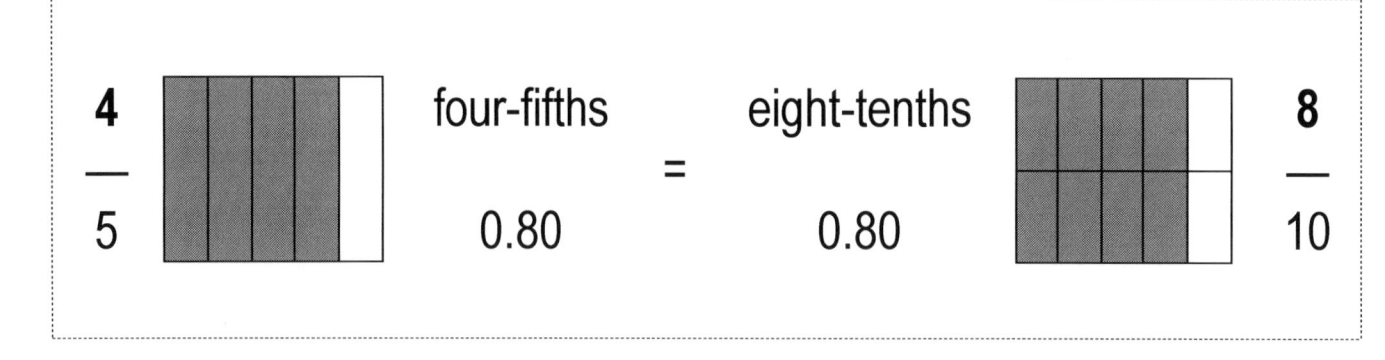

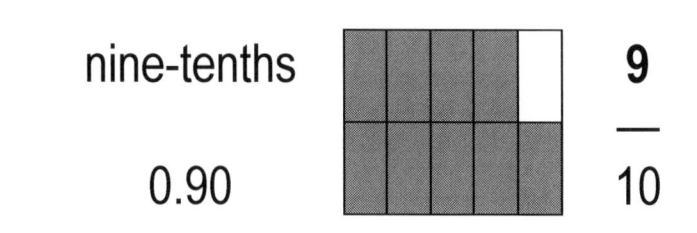

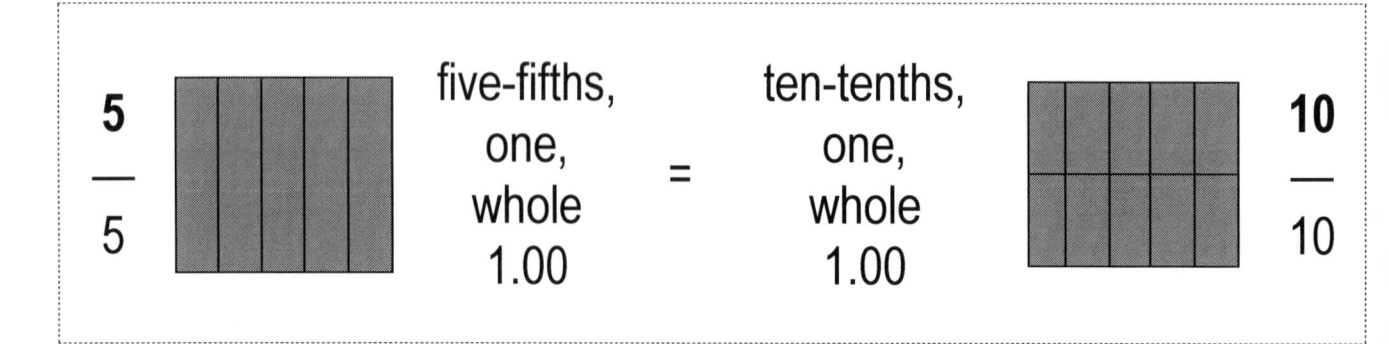

Fraction	Shape	Fraction Name / Decimal	→	Fraction Name / Decimal	Shape	Fraction

| | | | | seven-tenths 0.70 | | $\dfrac{7}{10}$ |

| $\dfrac{4}{5}$ | | four-fifths 0.80 | = | eight-tenths 0.80 | | $\dfrac{8}{10}$ |

| | | | | nine-tenths 0.90 | | $\dfrac{9}{10}$ |

| $\dfrac{5}{5}$ | | five-fifths, one, whole 1.00 | = | ten-tenths, one, whole 1.00 | | $\dfrac{10}{10}$ |

Thirds

| Shape / Fraction | → | Equivalent Shape / Equivalent Fraction | → | Decimal |

$\dfrac{0}{3}$ = $\dfrac{0}{1}$ = 0 = **0.00**

$\dfrac{1}{3}$ = 0.333

$\dfrac{2}{3}$ = 0.666

$\dfrac{3}{3}$ = $\dfrac{1}{1}$ = 1 = **1.00**

1) Sixths

Shape Fraction → Equivalent Shape(s) Equivalent Fraction(s) → Decimal

$\dfrac{0}{6}$ = $\dfrac{0}{3}$ = $\dfrac{0}{1}$ = 0

$\dfrac{1}{6}$ = 0.166

$\dfrac{2}{6}$ = $\dfrac{1}{3}$ = 0.333

54

2) **Sixths**

Shape Fraction →	Equivalent Shape Equivalent Fraction →	Decimal

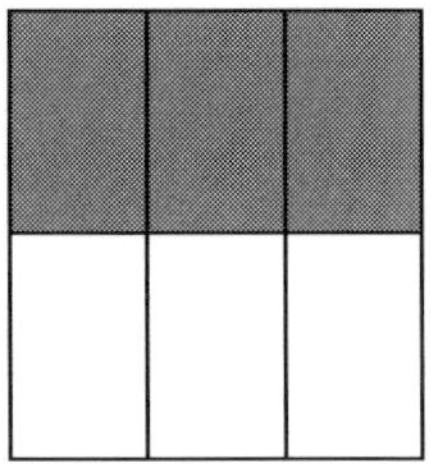

$\dfrac{3}{6} = \dfrac{1}{2} = 0.50$

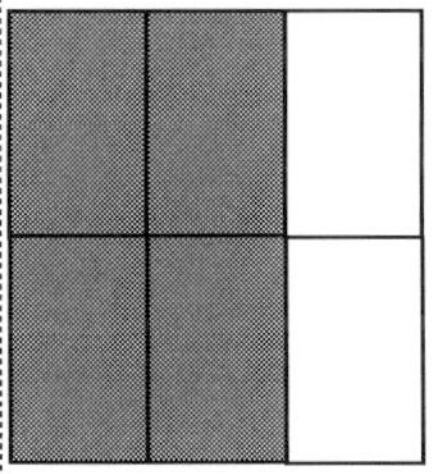

$\dfrac{4}{6} = \dfrac{2}{3} = 0.666$

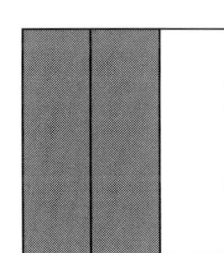

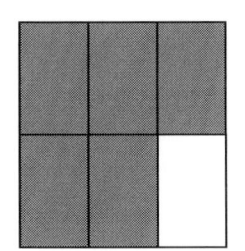

$\dfrac{5}{6} = 0.833$

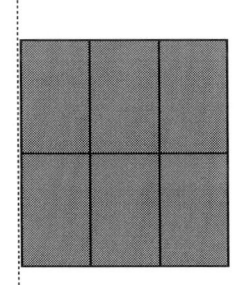

$\dfrac{6}{6} = \dfrac{3}{3} = \dfrac{1}{1} = 1.00$

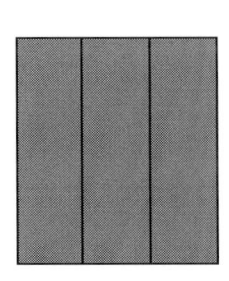

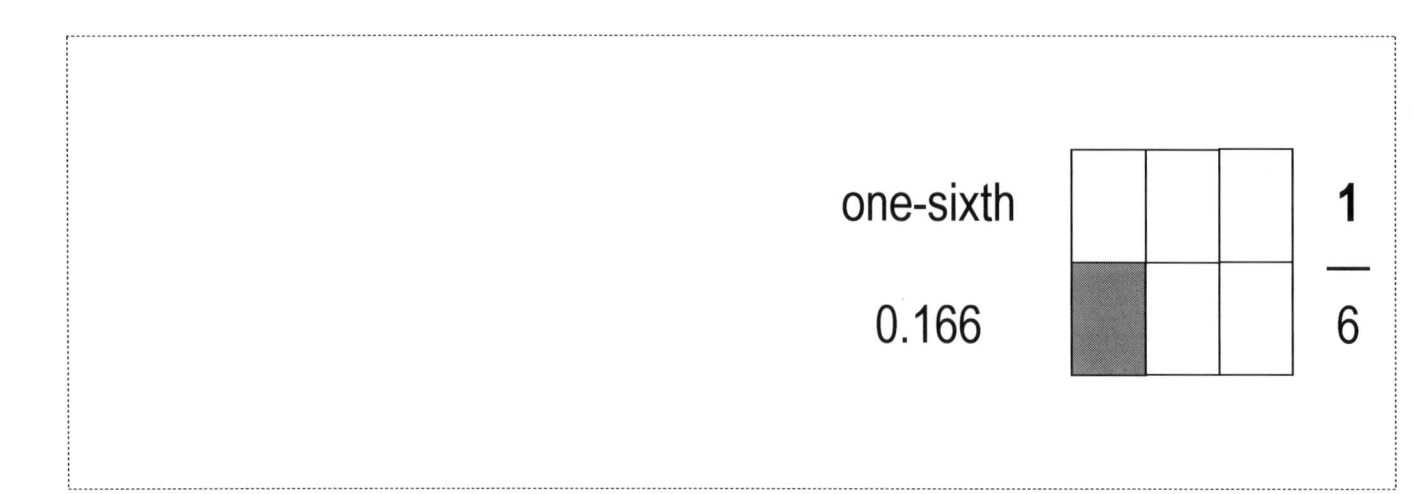

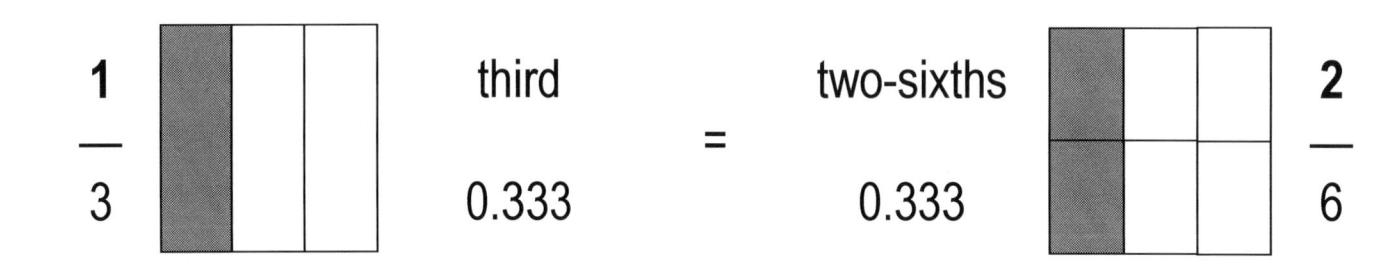

l) Thirds v Sixths

Fraction	Shape	Fraction Name / Decimal	→	Fraction Name / Decimal	Shape	Fraction

$\dfrac{0}{3}$ nothing 0   =   nothing 0 $\dfrac{0}{6}$

one-sixth   0.166 $\dfrac{1}{6}$

$\dfrac{1}{3}$ third   0.333   =   two-sixths   0.333 $\dfrac{2}{6}$

56

II) **Thirds** v **Sixths**

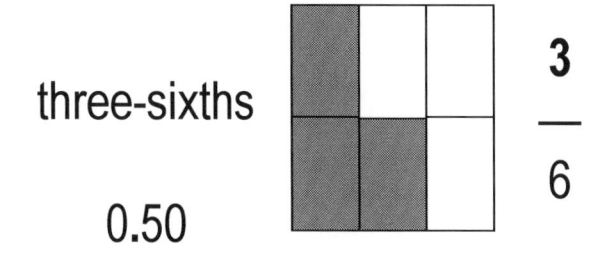

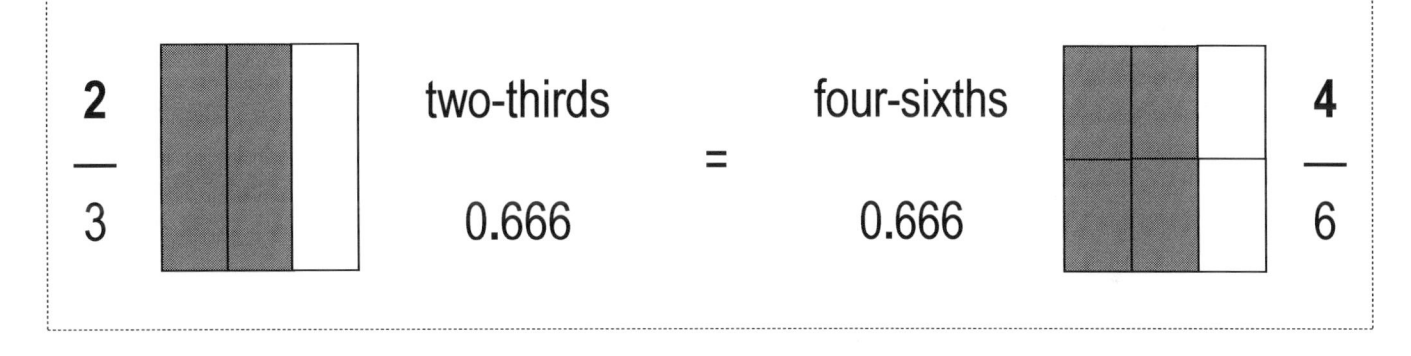

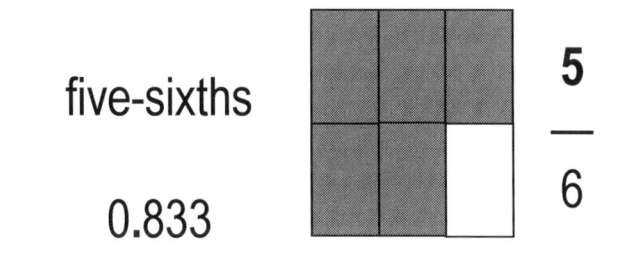

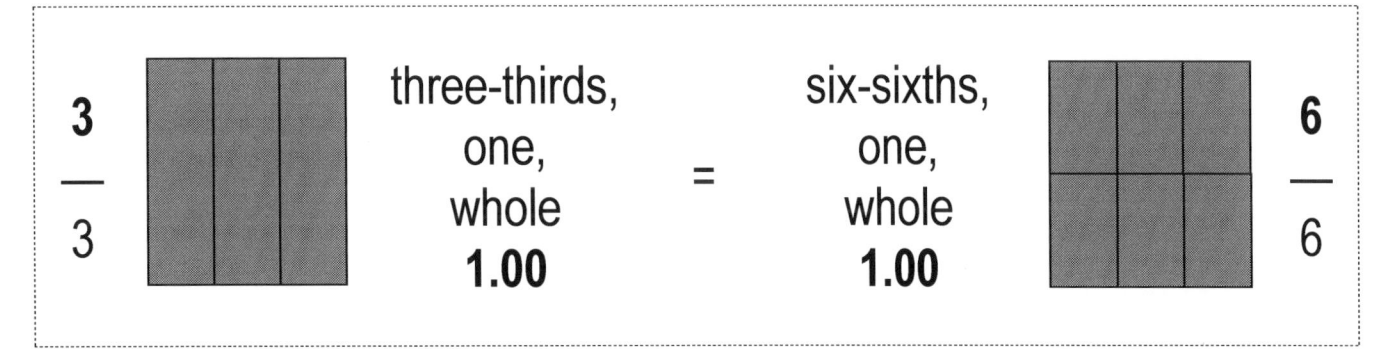

Fraction	Shape	Fraction Name / Decimal	→	Fraction Name / Decimal	Shape	Fraction
				three-sixths 0.50		$\dfrac{3}{6}$
$\dfrac{2}{3}$		two-thirds 0.666	=	four-sixths 0.666		$\dfrac{4}{6}$
				five-sixths 0.833		$\dfrac{5}{6}$
$\dfrac{3}{3}$		three-thirds, one, whole **1.00**	=	six-sixths, one, whole **1.00**		$\dfrac{6}{6}$

a) Ninths

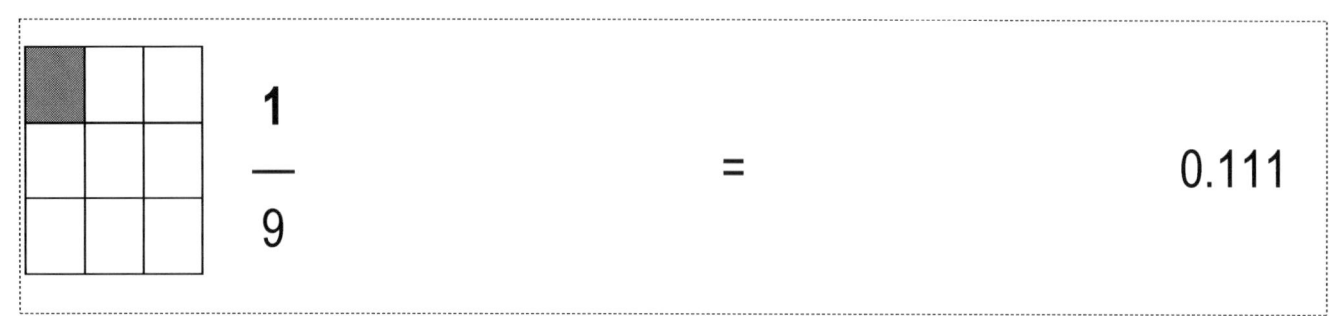

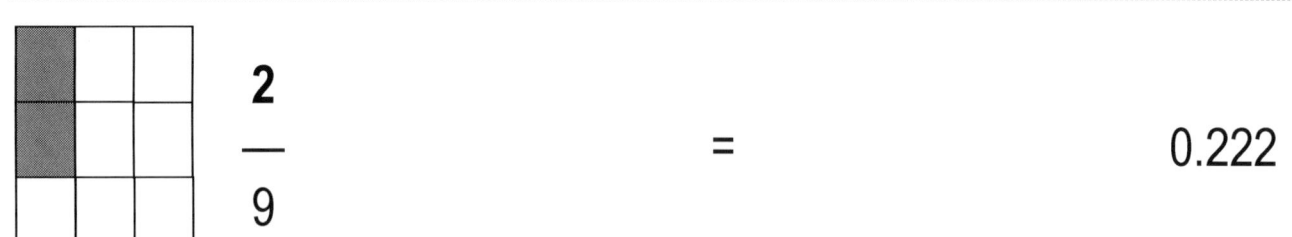

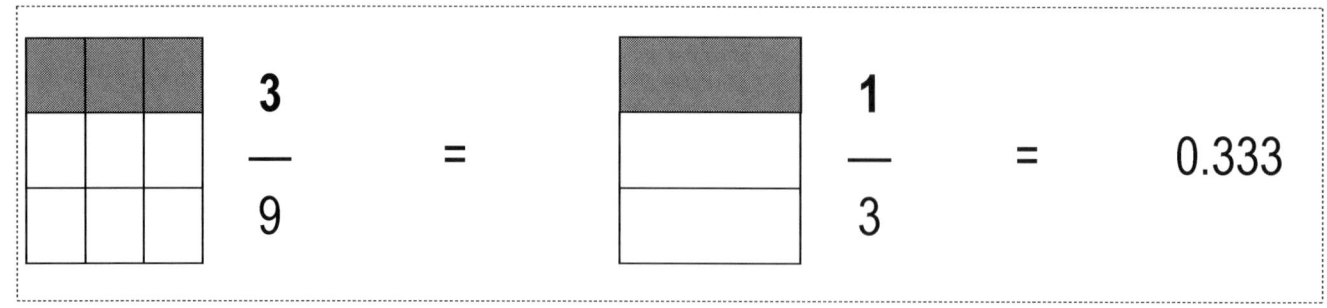

Shape Fraction	→	Shape Fraction	→	Shape Fraction	Decimal

$\dfrac{0}{9}$ = $\dfrac{0}{6}$ = $\dfrac{0}{3}$ = 0.00

$\dfrac{1}{9}$ = 0.111

$\dfrac{2}{9}$ = 0.222

$\dfrac{3}{9}$ = $\dfrac{1}{3}$ = 0.333

$\dfrac{4}{9}$ = 0.444

b) Ninths

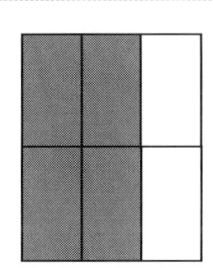

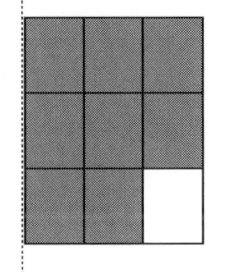

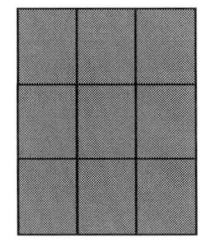

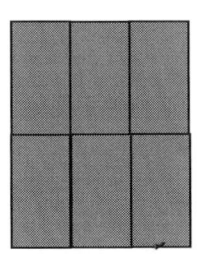

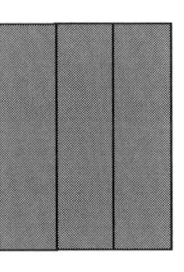

Shape Fraction	→	Shape Fraction	→	Shape Fraction	Decimal
$\dfrac{5}{9}$		=			0.555
$\dfrac{6}{9}$	=	$\dfrac{4}{6}$	=	$\dfrac{2}{3}$	= 0.666
$\dfrac{7}{9}$		=			0.777
$\dfrac{8}{9}$		=			0.888
$\dfrac{9}{9}$	=	$\dfrac{6}{6}$	=	$\dfrac{3}{3}$	= 1.00

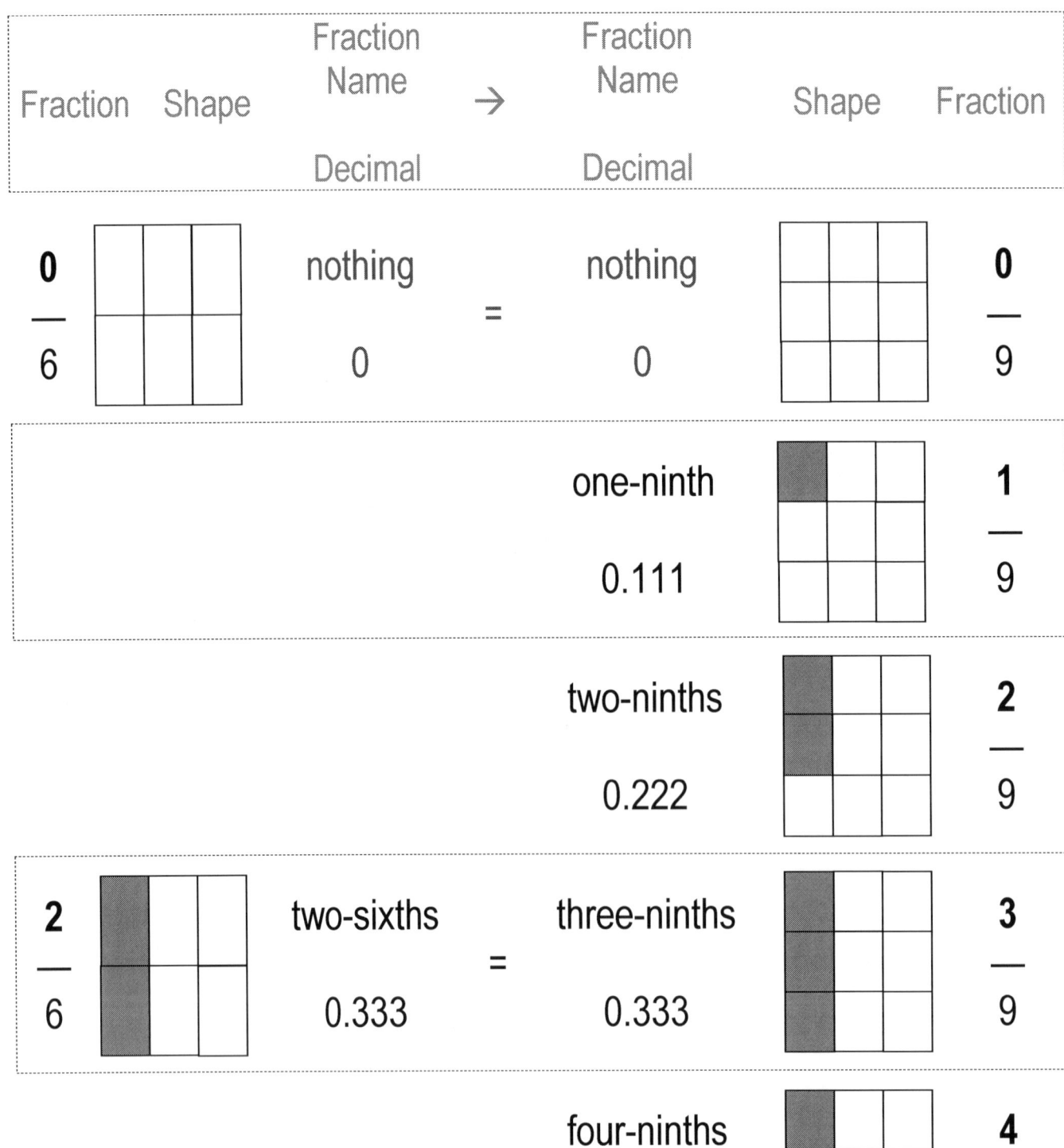

1) # Sixths v Ninths

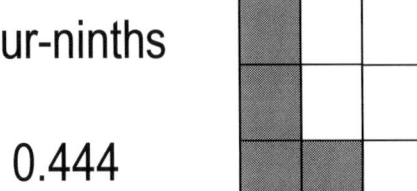

Fraction	Shape	Fraction Name / Decimal	→	Fraction Name / Decimal	Shape	Fraction
$\dfrac{0}{6}$		nothing / 0	=	nothing / 0		$\dfrac{0}{9}$
				one-ninth / 0.111		$\dfrac{1}{9}$
				two-ninths / 0.222		$\dfrac{2}{9}$
$\dfrac{2}{6}$		two-sixths / 0.333	=	three-ninths / 0.333		$\dfrac{3}{9}$
				four-ninths / 0.444		$\dfrac{4}{9}$

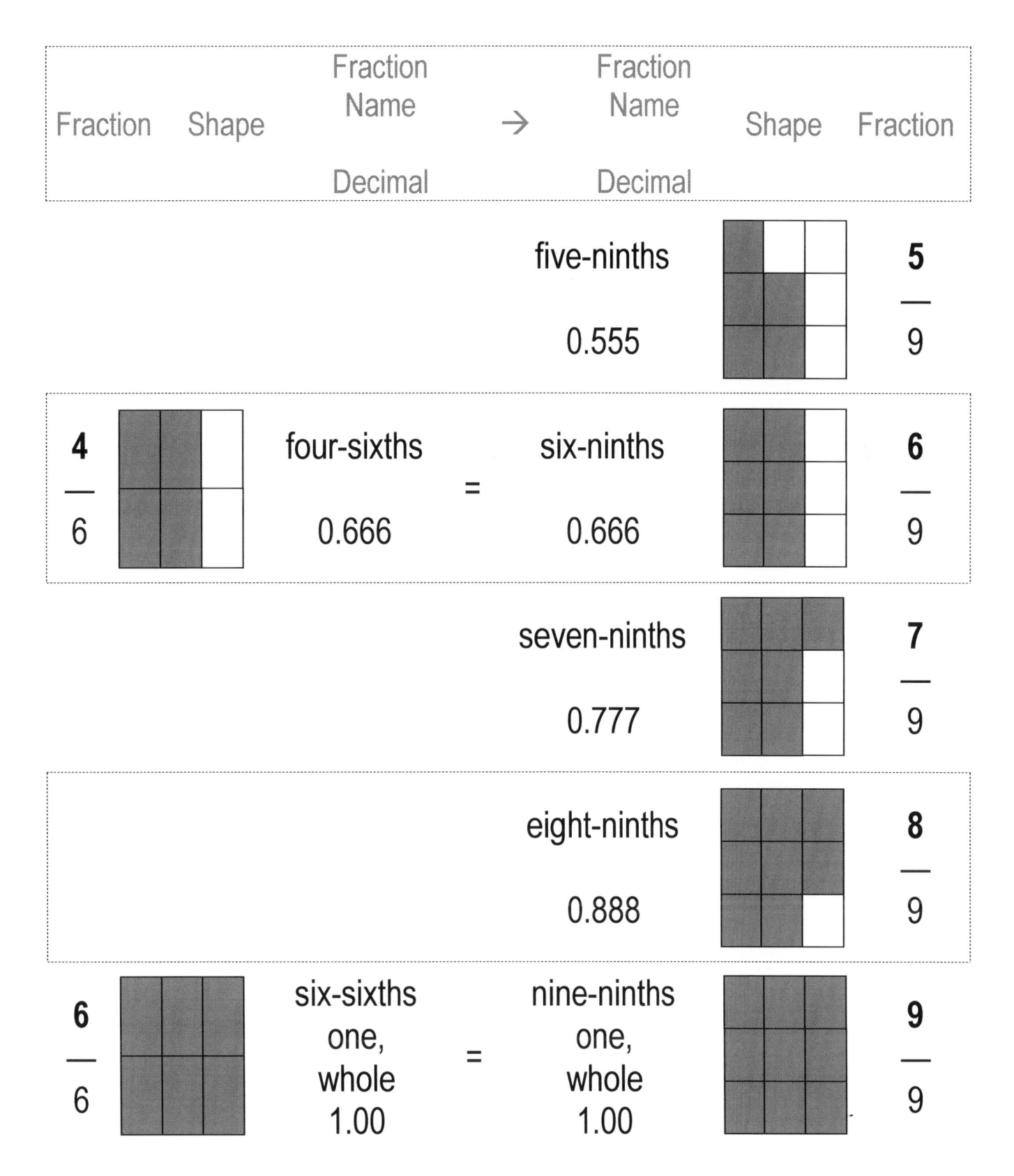

2) Sixths v Ninths

Fraction	Shape	Fraction Name / Decimal	→	Fraction Name / Decimal	Shape	Fraction
				five-ninths 0.555		$\dfrac{5}{9}$
$\dfrac{4}{6}$		four-sixths 0.666	=	six-ninths 0.666		$\dfrac{6}{9}$
				seven-ninths 0.777		$\dfrac{7}{9}$
				eight-ninths 0.888		$\dfrac{8}{9}$
$\dfrac{6}{6}$		six-sixths one, whole 1.00	=	nine-ninths one, whole 1.00		$\dfrac{9}{9}$

Thirds v Sixths v Ninths

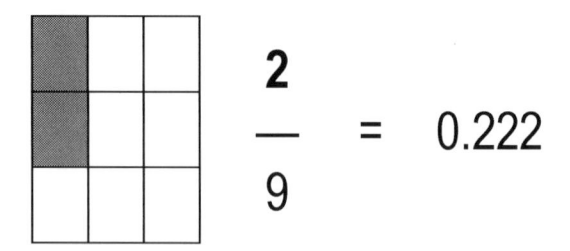

Fraction Shape	→	Fraction Shape	→	Shape Fraction	Decimal

$\dfrac{0}{3}$ = $\dfrac{0}{6}$ = $\dfrac{0}{9}$ = 0

$\dfrac{1}{9}$ = 0.111

$\dfrac{2}{9}$ = 0.222

$\dfrac{1}{3}$ = $\dfrac{2}{6}$ = $\dfrac{3}{9}$ = 0.333

$\dfrac{4}{9}$ = 0.444

62

II) Thirds v Sixths v Ninths

| Fraction / Shape | → | Fraction / Shape | → | Shape / Fraction | Decimal |

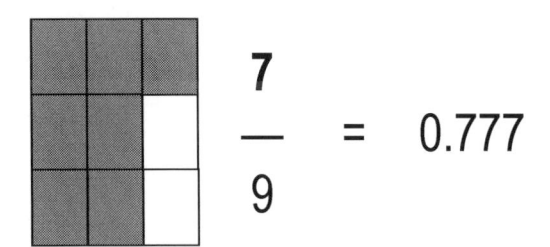

$\dfrac{5}{9}$ = 0.555

$\dfrac{2}{3}$ = $\dfrac{4}{6}$ = $\dfrac{6}{9}$ = 0.666

$\dfrac{7}{9}$ = 0.777

$\dfrac{8}{9}$ = 0.888

$\dfrac{3}{3}$ = $\dfrac{6}{6}$ = $\dfrac{9}{9}$ = 1.00

1) Equivalent **Fractions** and **Decimals**

These are fractions with the **same value** even though their **numerators** and **denominators** are **different**.

▽ *Halves, Quarters and Eighths*

Equivalent Fractions			Decimal
$\dfrac{0}{2} = \dfrac{0}{4} = \dfrac{0}{8}$	=		0
$\dfrac{1}{4} = \dfrac{2}{8}$	=		0.25
$\dfrac{1}{2} = \dfrac{2}{4} = \dfrac{4}{8}$	=		0.50
$\dfrac{3}{4} = \dfrac{6}{8}$	=		0.75
$\dfrac{2}{2} = \dfrac{4}{4} = \dfrac{8}{8}$	=		1.00

2) Equivalent **Fractions** and **Decimals**

◊ *Fifths and Tenths*

Equivalent Fractions		Decimal
$\dfrac{0}{5} = \dfrac{0}{10}$	=	0
$\dfrac{1}{5} = \dfrac{2}{10}$	=	0.20
$\dfrac{2}{5} = \dfrac{4}{10}$	=	0.40
$\dfrac{3}{5} = \dfrac{6}{10}$	=	0.60
$\dfrac{4}{5} = \dfrac{8}{10}$	=	0.80
$\dfrac{5}{5} = \dfrac{10}{10}$	=	**1.00**

3) Equivalent Fractions and Decimals

❏ *Thirds, Sixths and Ninths*

Equivalent Fractions			Decimal
$\dfrac{0}{3} = \dfrac{0}{6} = \dfrac{0}{9}$			= 0
$\dfrac{1}{6}$			= 0.166
$\dfrac{1}{3} = \dfrac{2}{6} = \dfrac{3}{9}$			= 0.333
$\dfrac{3}{6}$			= **0.50**
$\dfrac{2}{3} = \dfrac{4}{6} = \dfrac{6}{9}$			= 0.666
$\dfrac{5}{6}$			= 0.833
$\dfrac{3}{3} = \dfrac{6}{6} = \dfrac{9}{9}$			= **1.00**

Quiz 2

◁ Find the **odd one** out!

Which of the following numbers is **not** a fraction (*circle*)?

$$\frac{1}{2} \qquad \frac{1}{3}$$

$$\frac{1}{5} \qquad \frac{1}{4}$$

$$\frac{1}{6} \qquad \frac{1}{9}$$

$$\frac{1}{7} \qquad \frac{3}{4} \qquad \frac{1}{8}$$

$$\frac{1}{10} \qquad \frac{1}{1} \qquad 1$$

a) Fractions, **Decimals** and **Percentages**

▽ *Halves, Quarters and Eighths*

Fraction or Equivalent Fractions	Decimal	Percentage

$$\frac{0}{2} = \frac{0}{4} = \frac{0}{8} = 0.00 = 0\%$$

$$\frac{1}{8} = 0.125 = 12.5\%$$

$$\frac{1}{4} = \frac{2}{8} = 0.25 = 25\%$$

$$\frac{3}{8} = 0.375 = 37.5\%$$

b) # Fractions, **Decimals** and **Percentages**

▽ *Halves, Quarters and Eighths*

Fraction or Equivalent **Fractions**	**Decimal**	**Percentage**
$\frac{1}{2} = \frac{2}{4} = \frac{4}{8}$ =	0.50 =	50%
$\frac{5}{8}$ =	0.625 =	62.5%
$\frac{3}{4} = \frac{6}{8}$ =	0.75 =	75%
$\frac{7}{8}$ =	0.875 =	87.5%
$\frac{2}{2} = \frac{4}{4} = \frac{8}{8}$ =	1.00 =	100%

c) Fractions, **Decimals** and **Percentages**

◊ *Fifths and Tenths*

Fraction or Equivalent Fractions	Decimal	Percentage
$\frac{0}{5}$ = $\frac{0}{10}$	= 0.00	= 0%
$\frac{1}{10}$	= 0.10	= 10%
$\frac{1}{5}$ = $\frac{2}{10}$	= 0.20	= 20%
$\frac{3}{10}$	= 0.30	= 30%
$\frac{2}{5}$ = $\frac{4}{10}$	= 0.40	= 40%
$\frac{5}{10}$	= 0.50	= 50%

d) # Fractions, Decimals and Percentages

◊ *Fifths and Tenths*

Fraction or Equivalent **Fractions**	**Decimal**	**Percentage**
$\dfrac{3}{5} = \dfrac{6}{10} =$	$0.60 =$	60%
$\dfrac{7}{10} =$	$0.70 =$	70%
$\dfrac{4}{5} = \dfrac{8}{10} =$	$0.80 =$	80%
$\dfrac{9}{10} =$	$0.90 =$	90%
$\dfrac{5}{5} = \dfrac{10}{10} =$	$1.00 =$	100%

e) Fractions, **Decimals** and **Percentages**

Thirds, Sixths and Ninths

Fraction or Equivalent **Fractions**	Decimal	Percentage
$\frac{0}{3} = \frac{0}{6} = \frac{0}{9}$ =	0.00 =	0%
$\frac{1}{9}$ =	0.111 =	11.1%
$\frac{2}{9}$ =	0.222 =	22.2%
$\frac{1}{3} = \frac{2}{6} = \frac{3}{9}$ =	0.333 =	33.3%
$\frac{4}{9}$ =	0.444 =	44.4%

f) Fractions, **Decimals** and **Percentages**

Thirds, Sixths and Ninths

Fraction or Equivalent **Fractions**			Decimal	Percentage
		$\frac{5}{9}$ =	0.555 =	55.5%
$\frac{2}{3}$ = $\frac{4}{6}$ =		$\frac{6}{9}$ =	0.666 =	66.6%
		$\frac{7}{9}$ =	0.777 =	77.7%
		$\frac{8}{9}$ =	0.888 =	88.8%
$\frac{3}{3}$ = $\frac{6}{6}$ =		$\frac{9}{9}$ =	1.00 =	100%

Copyright © Eng S Jama
All rights reserved.

eng-s-jama@hotmail.com

Also, available in **colour** ebooks and **workbooks**

--- Other titles in this series ---

- Adding **Fractions** *Visually*
Second Edition
Colour

- Adding *More* **Fractions** *Step-by-step*
Second Edition
Colour

Thank You for buying my book and helping the author.
I hope you have enjoyed reading it.
If so, please, leave a good review (the more stars the merrier!).
If not, please, send your feedback, comments and corrections to:
eng-s-jama@hotmail.com. Thanks.

Answers and explanation from pages 5 to 6.

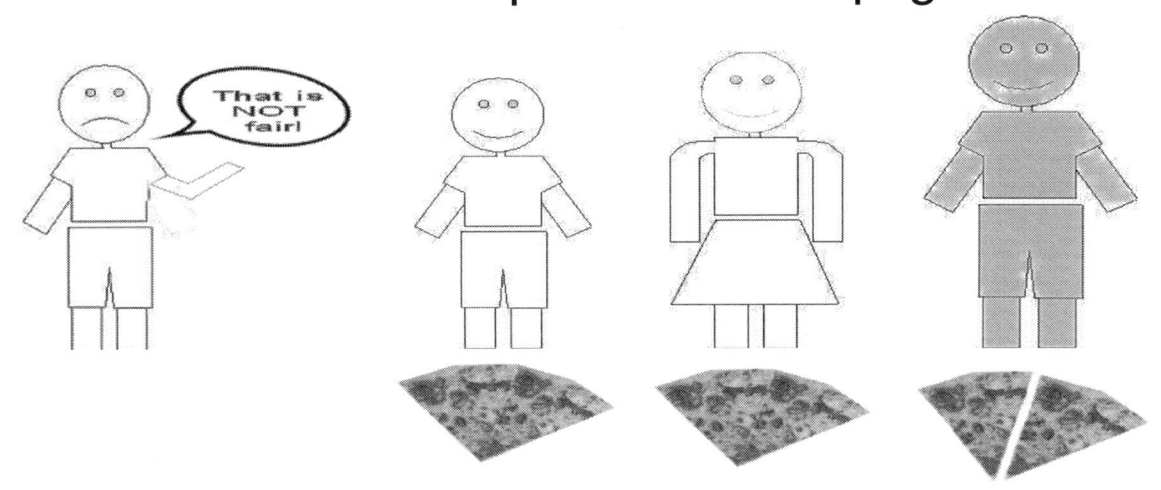

Why was the younger boy not happy?
He thought his older brother had more pizza!

The younger boy had 1 big slice ($\frac{1}{3}$ of the whole pizza).

The older boy had 2 small slices – each half of the size of that of his younger brother ($\frac{1}{6} + \frac{1}{6} = \frac{2}{6} = \frac{1}{3}$ of the whole pizza!)

The girl also got 1 big slice ($\frac{1}{3}$ of the whole pizza).

So, they all had the same amount of pizza!

($\frac{1}{3} + \frac{1}{3} + \frac{1}{3} = \frac{3}{3}$ = 1 whole pizza).

What could be the problem?
The younger boy did not understand fair sharing in fractions!

The solution was to swap the pizzas.
The younger boy thought he had more pizza when he got 2 small pizzas (from his older brother)!

But he still had the same amount of pizza ($\frac{1}{3}$ of the whole pizza).

Understanding Fractions *Visually*
Second Edition

- ***Visually*** teaches young children etc **shape** and **fraction** association.

- *Illustrated* with shaded **shapes** to develop learner's understanding of fundamental maths fractions.

- Introduces and extensively employs the principle of **equivalent fractions** and **decimals**, as well as, **whole numbers** using shaded **shapes**.

Compares **fractions, decimals** and **percentages**.

- Brief **introductions** to **fractions** and **equivalent fractions** plus **quick quizzes** to check learner's understanding and progress!

Uses *easy* language and plenty of shaded **shapes**, *simple* **maths language** and **fractions vocabulary**.

Printed by Amazon Italia Logistica S.r.l.
Torrazza Piemonte (TO), Italy